CRACKING
— *the* —
FOUNTAIN OF
YOUTH
— CODE —

A WOMAN'S GUIDE TO BEING HEALTHIER, HAPPIER AND EMPOWERED FOR LIFE

MONICA DIAZ CAMPBELL

Copyright © 2019 by Monica Diaz Campbell

All rights reserved. No part of this book may be reproduced in any form without permission in writing from the author. Reviewers may quote brief passages in reviews.

Publishing services provided by Archangel Ink

ISBN-13: 978-1-950043-04-0

ACKNOWLEDGEMENTS

This book is a pouring out of love.

The challenge, for me, is ensuring I acknowledge all who have influenced me in my life and in some way contributed to the content of this book.

I firmly believe we are all teachers for one another.

To my first teacher, my mother, Terri Chamberlain.

She sacrificed much of her life for what she believed was best for her children.

My mom was the most beautiful woman I have ever known.

I only wish she could have seen herself through my eyes.

This would have allowed her to know and feel her true beauty while she was alive.

In her passing, she taught me pure love.

Thank you mamacita.

I love you always.

To my pops, Harry M. Chamberlain.

I am immensely grateful for all the experiences and memories we have been fortunate to share with one another.

It is because of your influence I have strived to know and be more.

As a child, I could not have imagined how wonderful our relationship could be as grown adults.

Thank you for being my advisor, friend, and confidant.

I love you so much.

To my fabulous loving husband, Jay Campbell.

Baby, I knew the moment we embraced our lives together were destined for greatness.

Your heart spoke to mine and it has not let me down.

Thank you for reminding me of our greatness when I doubted.

Thank you for being my best friend and lover.

I know and experience more of life because of you.

Thank you for introducing me to REAL health and fitness from a physical perspective and anchoring our love from a spiritual perspective.

Thank you for helping edit this book even though I have had some little complaints.

I truly appreciate all you do for me and our family.

I am so in love with you and the life we live.

To my children.

Evan, thank you for teaching me how to love you and showing me the art of acceptance.

Ezra, thank you for teaching me the importance of integrity and showing me how to love unconditionally.

Alana, thank you for being my first practice shot of raising a little girl.

I knew before you were born, you would have a life of adventure.

Life with you is definitely more fun.

Alex, little did I know how much I would learn from my first bonus daughter.

You were my first experience with a feminine little girl.

Thank you for your patience with me and allowing me to love you.

Gabbi, my fellow **sag**(itarius), your smile is infectious.

We are so alike yet so different.

My wish is for you to know the world is for you not against you.

I love you and am so grateful we get to practice the game of life together.

For each one of my children, may you each see yourselves with eyes of love and know you are deeply loved always.

To all of my mentors, clients and friends throughout my life, THANK YOU!

A special mention to Matthew Ferry for teaching me how to design, achieve and live an epic life.

A special Thank you to Tom Zakharov for his ninja editing and copy writing skills.

To Matt Lawrence for his graphic artist mastery.

To Max Mackson for his jedi technology skill.

Every person I have come in contact with has allowed me to learn and grow.

Through both the good and challenging times, I have observed how events shape us.

I live every day in full appreciation of my amazing life.

Let's all commit to living and being our best selves at any age :)

CRACKING THE FOUNTAIN OF YOUTH CODE

My Dear Beautiful Sister:

When you look in the mirror, what do you see?

Are you allowing age to define you? Age doesn't define you.

Your beauty and worth defines you. But wait, doesn't beauty and worth diminish as we age?

Nope. I am speaking of a beauty and worth beneath the exterior. A beauty which exists because you are you. A sense of worth because you feel good to be you.

Do you KNOW and FEEL how beautiful and worthy you are?

STOP whatever you are doing, read and FEEL these words....

I AM BEAUTIFUL.   **I HAVE WORTH.**

I AM BEAUTIFUL.   **I HAVE WORTH.**

I AM BEAUTIFUL.   **I HAVE WORTH.**

I AM BEAUTIFUL. I HAVE WORTH

As we journey together throughout the pages, my intention is for you to know and feel your own beauty and worth, both inside and out.

Feeling your beauty allows you to feel and be worthy. When you feel worthy, then you will allow yourself to "Crack the Fountain of Youth Code".

Please understand: I am not asking you to be conceited or arrogant.

I am not attempting to convince you that you are better than anyone else.

We are all connected. We are all one. We are all beautifully and intentionally created.

My desire is for you to know your true beauty and discover who you are beneath your skin suit.

When one recognizes their beauty within, one can fully appreciate the beauty in others.

When one knows and appreciates their own worth, one can know and appreciate the value of others.

Appreciating the beauty and value in others allows us all to live in a better, more beautiful world.

I am filled with appreciation to be on this journey with you.

Let's get cracking and have some fun!

Love,

Monica

CONTENTS

INTRODUCTION 1

CHAPTER 1
ACCEPTANCE 11

CHAPTER 2
EMBRACE YOUR INNER GODDESS 35

CHAPTER 3
LOVE FULLY 63

CHAPTER 4
LOOK FOR EVIDENCE 75

CHAPTER 5
REDEFINE/RELEASE YOUR PAST 97

CHAPTER 6
FORGIVE AND RELEASE RESENTMENTS 113

CHAPTER 7
THERE IS NO COMPARISON 133

CHAPTER 8
MANAGE STRESS 149

CHAPTER 9
GRATITUDE & APPRECIATION 161

CHAPTER 10
ARE YOU MAKING YOURSELF OLDER & SICKER? 175

CHAPTER 11
SILENCE & SOLITUDE 187

CHAPTER 12
MINDFULNESS, MEDITATION & PRAYER 195

CHAPTER 13
HEAL FROM WITHIN 209

CHAPTER 14
THE POWER OF TOUCH 225

CHAPTER 15
BREATHING 231

CHAPTER 16
GROUNDING 245

CHAPTER 17
WORK YOUR BODY 253

CHAPTER 18
FOOD 269

CHAPTER 19
HORMONES 293

CHAPTER 20
SLEEP 305

CHAPTER 21
HAVE FUN 313

CHAPTER 22
CONTRIBUTION (PASS YOUR GODDESS TORCH) 321

CONCLUSION 327

A SINCERE REQUEST 331

ABOUT THE AUTHORS 333

INTRODUCTION

Remember what it was like to be a little girl?

I am referring to the little girl who was innocent and filled with life.

Before you were conditioned by well intentioned parents, family members, and/or society.

Your imagination could take you anywhere and you could be anything.

All seemed possible.

Getting old was so far away. Perhaps you even felt indestructible.

But as you have gotten older, do you feel like you have lost your child-like wonder and curiosity?

Does life seem more like a chore?

If so, you may be longing to rediscover that wonder.

You may be searching for the joy and ease of life?

You may be seeking this joy outside of yourself because you lost it from within.

If life does not seem like a chore but you feel like something is missing, learn to play and have more fun.

Playing and having fun with life helps you realize that "little girl" is still inside of you!

This little childlike girl still desires to laugh and play.

She wants YOU to remember how beautiful and worthy she is.

This little girl is timeless - she will forever and always be a part of you.

When you look in the mirror, what do you see?

Is the reflection showing you an older woman?

Do you see the reflection of an older woman with wrinkles and "imperfections".

Where is the beauty?

If you look closely, perhaps you see the dark circles under your eyes or the discoloration of your skin.

Is the skin on your face and/or body sagging?

What is the first thought that comes to mind?

"Me, as timeless?

Uggh, I am SO old and unattractive!"

What happened?

Time has passed and life happened.

Challenges have knocked you down.

The worries of life have shown up as worry lines all over your face.

Your skin sags. Your hair has fallen out and lacks its luster.

What is one to do if the curse of aging has wreaked havoc in one's reality?

CAN I DEFEAT THE "CURSE" OF AGING?

If you think aging is a curse then there is no way to defeat it.

My first suggestion would be to look at aging as a gift.

Aging is a process where your body/mind/spirit goes through a complete transformation.

INTRODUCTION

You get to choose whether this transformation is positive or negative.

If you were to look at your own life, what are you doing to age better?

Buying expensive creams?

Botox/Fillers/Laser Treatments? Facelift?

Making sure to get your hair colored every 2 weeks?

Are you doing your best to combat signs of aging?

If you think aging is just about what you look like, then it is easy to believe it a curse.

Believing aging is a curse, will cause you to think it is downright scary.

Think about it for a minute.

Why do you think most women think the following:
- Aging has become the #1 enemy of women.
- Aging is something to prepare for.
- Aging is something to fight and something to resist.
- Aging is an inconvenience and something to hide.
- Age is something to dismiss through beliefs like "if I act like I am not getting older, then I won't be."
- Looking younger is better.

When I ask "Google" for the definition of 'aging', it states:
1. (noun): The process of growing old.
2. (adjective): (of a person): growing old; elderly

Growing old and being elderly...NO THANK YOU!

What does most of society believe happens to someone as they grow old?

- Disease
- Loneliness
- Becoming less able to move and function
- Death
- Wrinkles
- Loss of Hair
- Memory Loss

Is this really what happens to EVERYONE?

Or are we conditioned to believe aging is essentially a 'death sentence'?

No matter what you believe right now, I'd like to propose a friendly thought experiment.

Something for you to keep in mind as you read the pages of this book:

> From this moment forward, allow yourself to view aging from a different perspective (even if you don't believe it at first).
>
> Give yourself permission to be open to a new and entirely different message I am about to deliver to you.
>
> I can already hear what is going on in some of your minds, and that's perfectly ok! Breaking our deeply ingrained beliefs is no easy feat, and it takes both time and patience.
>
> But if you are truly committed to embracing every aspect of your feminine beauty and worth I ask you to squash your old conditioning patterns about the 'death' sentence of 'aging' and re-contextualize how you define the word.

I am not saying we won't get older.

Please don't misunderstand my message.

INTRODUCTION

Our bodies will change and eventually physical vessel death will occur.

This is inevitable.

Time passes no matter what we do.

As of the time this book gets released into the world, nobody has found a way to stop it.

The purpose of my book is to provide another perspective on aging.

And to teach women to enjoy the process, rather than fight and struggle against it.

It is time for you to be in control of who you are and HOW you age.

It is time for you to embrace the beautiful being who is YOU!

The best way to get started on the journey towards beauty is to begin having 'conversations' with ourselves.

Ask questions to yourself and see what answers come to you.

Don't believe me because I wrote this book.

This is about YOU and how you decide to age.

You are the author of your own book and it's called "Your Life".

Here are some questions you can ask yourself (feel free to come up with your own) as you read through the pages of my book.

I highly recommend you do this, because it will put you in a more empowered state to take action.

You will become better connected with strengthening perspectives that make embracing your youth a natural and effortless outcome:

- Is there such a thing as a Fountain of Youth?
- Is this true for me?

- How does this make me feel?
- Have I noticed this in my own life?
- How am I aging?
- Am I scared to get older?
- What scares me about getting older?
- How can I implement this in my own life?
- Am I ready to make positive changes which will allow me to crack the "fountain of youth" code?
- Do I like the way I look?
- Do I like the way if FEEL?

WHAT IS THE REAL DEFINITION OF "FOUNTAIN OF YOUTH"?

As you read this book, you will learn how to crack your own "fountain of youth" code.

You will be able to tap into the healthier, happier and empowered version of you, no matter what physical age you are.

But what exactly do I mean by the term 'Fountain of Youth'?

I define "foundation of youth" as being in a state where you are being youthful, beautiful, and filled with energy.

Merriam Webster defines "fountain of youth" as: a fountain with magic water which when drunk will cause a person to live forever.

I want you to pretend the words in the pages of this book are your magic water.

This water when consumed and felt (or spoken out loud with conviction), will cause you to live youthfully and forever with an abundant reservoir of energy.

INTRODUCTION

In writing 'Cracking the Fountain of Youth Code', my #1 goal is to help women find ways to age gracefully while being sexy, fit, and happier.

To put more life into YOUR years.

I am not implying I can give you answers on how NOT to age.

Nor can I teach you how to look like you are in your 20s when you are in your 60s.

I don't have a magic elixir or pill to turn you into a younger version of yourself.

As I said before, time will inevitably pass and your body will change.

Your physical body will pass away and eventually become dust.

The life you have in your remaining physical years is entirely up to you.

For some, the term "fountain of youth" is foreign because the reality you currently live in tells you otherwise.

You feel old, tired, moody and you just don't get around like you once did.

This can make it challenging for you to believe there is a way to be and feel younger.

Ironically, being younger starts with how you view yourself and the world around you.

When you walk around and see older women, what do you typically see?

You can see an emptiness, sadness and regret in the faces and body language of many women today.

It seems many have given up, as their entire vibe screams, "My time has passed".

And it's no wonder!

We live in a time where healthcare has become "Sick Care".

It is not about being healthy, at least not anymore.

Instead, it's about avoiding sickness or treating symptoms with pharmaceutical medications.

Sure, we are told to get our yearly mammogram, but we aren't told about whether a mammogram is the best way to detect breast cancer.

Interestingly enough, most women are not even given the option for a thermography.

HMO's, PPO's (insurance companies), and the pharmaceutical companies run the medical system more than well intentioned physicians.

Even the best doctors are trained by the pharmaceutical companies in much of their schooling.

It has become much more about corporate profits then doing what is best for the patient.

INTRODUCTION

So what can you do?

You can start by reading inspirational books like this one to teach you the awareness necessary to better show up in your own life.

Stop allowing yourself to fall prey to a medical system and society that wants you to depend on it so it can thrive while you are depleted - (emotionally, physically and financially).

Above all else, I ask that you truly value YOU and promise to finish this book.

I surround you in love as you take this journey with me.

And remember:

YOU are more powerful AND BEAUTIFUL than you realize.

YES, you are WORTHY!

CHAPTER 1
ACCEPTANCE

"Notice the stiffest tree is most easily cracked while the bamboo or willow survives by bending with the wind."
–Bruce Lee

Aging is similar to the quote which begins this chapter.

But what is aging, really?

It is the passage of time and its effects relative to the care you've shown your body.

Each of our bodies will go through changes as time passes.

NO MATTER WHAT YOU DO, your body does change.

NO MATTER WHAT YOU DO, your skin will change.

Aging (getting older) is part of a natural biological process.

When we accept the changes that occur with getting older, we allow our body to progress without resistance.

Resistance to aging, manifests as stiffness in the body.

Think of resistance as poison to your body.

Resistance builds pockets of blocked energy.

Resistance is expressed as sickness and/or disease.

Especially when it is held onto for long periods of time.

These pockets of blocked energy do not allow the energy to flow through your body.

Your body functions best when there is flow. (For Example: If your blood does not flow easily through your body, it creates blood clots.)

Avoiding sickness and disease, is often determined by how well one is at releasing resistance.

To be clear, the information in this book is not about whether or not you will age.

It is more about HOW will you age.

How you age depends on how you take care of yourself physically, emotionally, and spiritually.

ACCEPTANCE VERSUS RESISTANCE (OR HOW TO PERCEIVE AGING IN A HEALTHY, BLISSFUL WAY)

As time passes, acceptance of this fact (aging depends on how you take care of yourself) brings freedom.

ACCEPTANCE

Freedom allows one to feel empowered and capable of overcoming the resistance blocks of life and getting older

The thought of getting older can sound scary

Especially when we look around and see so many women falling apart as they get older.

We see women battling obesity, depression, cancer, osteoporosis, etc.

Seeing women battle these issues can cause major resistance.

It becomes easy to fear what the future could look like as we age.

We can think to ourselves "I don't want to experience that when I get older".

What we don't realize, are the habits these other people have created to get to where they are.

The only journey you have some control over is your own.

Remember what it was like to be in your 20s and think how old 40 sounded?

I remember thinking life would be over in my 40s.

I remember throwing out my sexy clothes in my mid 30's thinking there would be no way I could ever wear "those" clothes again.

Little did I know, life begins at the exact moment and time one decides it.

Acceptance of aging is but one component.

The other is acceptance of WHO you are.

If you are comfortable in your own skin, then it makes aging more enjoyable.

This can be extremely challenging for many women.

We will discuss self-love tips later in the book.

Some women look at themselves and wish they looked better, prettier, skinnier, fuller, and many other things.

They have grown accustomed to breaking themselves down, rather than appreciating who they are.

So how can you age effectively, when you don't even like who you are?

STOP being your own worst enemy.

Every moment brings an opportunity to accept and love who we are, regardless of our perceived imperfections.

Aging does NOT have to mean the end of beauty and grace.

With age, more beauty and wisdom comes our way.

We tend to allow the negative events of our life to take hold and break us down.

This makes us feel older than we actually are.

Why do we hold onto these things when they clearly won't benefit us?

ACCEPTANCE

Note on the above picture:

My biological grandmother-the woman next to my dad in the middle on the left hand side (wearing a blue blouse)-resented my Grandma Dyne-on her immediate right (blouse with polka dots) for well over 30 years.

My grandfather (in the white shirt) was married to my grandmother then divorced while my father was in his teens.

My Grandma Dyne and grandmother had been friends until my Grandma Dyne and grandfather came out expressing their love for one another.

You can tell by the expression on my grandmother's face, she did not want to be sitting at the same table as my Grandma Dyne and grandfather.

It was unfortunate because my grandmother chose to hold onto this resentment until she died in her 70s.

She aged quickly and unhappily.

It's not aging that breaks us down.

It is how we view and deal with all the events in our life.

Holding pain inside harms us.

Acting like something doesn't bother us, creates stress in the body.

We don't want to feel hurt.

We resist the pain and act like it doesn't exist, even though it eats us up on the inside.

The sweet irony is that holding onto pain is what depletes beauty and grace.

My mentor Matthew Ferry once taught me something profound.

It completely transformed the way I perceived aging:

"What you resist persists.

What you accept transforms"

Think about it for a minute.

We are taught to resist nearly everything.

"Fight Aging", "Battle Cancer", "F@$k Cancer", and the list goes on.

Why do we have to fight or battle anything?

Acceptance doesn't mean you give up.

It means you let go of any attachment to what you think it "should" look like.

Acceptance gives you a clean slate to work with and heal from.

If you have cancer or disease, the first step could be, "I accept my body has this illness and is speaking to me."

Acceptance doesn't mean you are thinking, "Thank God, I have cancer and I am this cancer.".

It also doesn't mean, "Oh well, I have cancer and I am gonna die"

You are NOT and never will be your disease.

The disease is simply providing feedback to you.

The feedback can be anything.

For example:

- My body has cancer and it has shown me how to fully appreciate life.

ACCEPTANCE

- Before I was diagnosed, I thought my life was meaningless. I now know my life has meaning and I value it. I choose to live.
- My body is breaking down and I never appreciated my body. I always looked at what was wrong with my body. Thank you for showing me I have so much to appreciate about my body.
- Miracles really do exist. I am a walking miracle.

If you are a woman in your mid 40s and are scared of what you will look and feel like in your 50s and 60s, join the crowd.

Society conditions you to fight aging.

Afterall, you gotta prepare for the worst.

"Anti-aging" products are a MULTI-BILLION dollar business.

You buy expensive face creams, get Botox/fillers, and start looking into plastic surgery with the 'hope' you look youthful as you get older.

Deep down, you are dreading the possibility of looking older.

If you are going to buy expensive creams, get Botox/fillers and undergo plastic surgery, then enjoy the process.

Accept the fact you are getting older.

Be OK with it.

LOVE and BE KIND to yourself.

If you decide to buy your face creams and/or Botox/fillers, do it because it is what YOU truly desire to do for you.

NOT because society is telling you to.

So many women have been conditioned to believe their value is held in their physical appearance.

God forbid if we should actually look old.

We all go through it at some point in our life.

Dreading the possibility of looking like a worn out old lady.

There is such freedom in acceptance.

You are releasing negative energetic chains from your soul.

These chains hold you back from fully experiencing your life (i.e. resistance).

ACCEPTANCE IS KEY.

Acceptance allows us to move into this present moment with true freedom and peace.

I want you to think of resistance and acceptance like this:
- Squeeze your arm as tight and as long as you can.
- Let go once you feel like it hurts.
- Can you feel the circulation being cut off? It's crazy how it can even tingle after you let go because your blood begins to circulate again. The lack of circulation is resistance. It stops the flow.

Acceptance relieves resistance.

It allows flow.

It is an experience of ease.

Another form of resistance is wrinkles.

The more you resist aging, the more wrinkles show up.

I like to think of wrinkles as "worry lines".

Too much sun exposure, smoking and other external factors can bring wrinkles too.

But resistance can bring even more wrinkles.

Let's get real, stressing about not stressing won't help either.

Stop acting like you won't get older, because the hard truth is every day you are getting older.

When my oldest son was younger, I remember he hated celebrating anyone's birthday.

He felt like it was a day we all made up and he didn't feel like participating.

This could have been his teenage angst attempting to ruffle feathers.

But he offered a profound insight which has stayed with me:

"A birthday just tells you you are another day closer to death".

As morbid as that might sound to some, it is true.

My pops continually reminds me,

"Honey, today I am the oldest that I've ever been and today I am the youngest I will ever be."

If you could look at getting older from a different perspective, would you actually enjoy the process of aging better?

Enjoy yourself at any age.

You won't ever be that age again in this lifetime.

PRACTICING COMPLETE ACCEPTANCE OF WHO YOU ARE AT ANY AGE YOU HAPPEN TO BE

We are all an accumulation of patterned thinking throughout our lifetime.

Every morning, you are more than likely doing the same thing in the same way.

You have conditioned yourself to get up and go to the bathroom and/or brush your teeth.

It is almost like you can do it without even thinking.

This is conditioned and patterned behavior.

You could probably do it without putting much thought into it.

How you speak to yourself is similar.

You have trained yourself to be your own best friend or your own worst enemy.

If you were brought up in a home where worry, stress and fear drove your reaction to circumstances, acceptance is challenging.

ACCEPTANCE

It is easier to stress about a situation than it is to learn how to maneuver through it.

It is easier to worry about things falling apart than it is to put effort into creating the perfect life.

Does it mean you are hopeless? NO!

Acceptance of getting older begins with a simple acknowledgement:

"Yes, time passes, change is the only constant in life and all is well."

Let's practice:

> **"Yes, time passes, change is the only constant in life and all is well"**
>
> **"Yes, time passes, change is the only constant in life and all is well."**
>
> **"Yes, time passes, change is the only constant in life and all is well."**
>
> **"Yes, time passes, change is the only constant in life and all is well."**
>
> **"Yes, time passes, change is the only constant in life and all is well."**

Each time you say it, hopefully it feels better and true for you.

If it doesn't, then it's OK.

It simply means it may take a bit longer for you to reach a state of acceptance.

This is your life.

You get to live it any way you choose.

You can resist getting older through struggle.

Or you can accept getting older while creating the best possible version of you.

The choice is truly yours.

LEARNING HOW TO ACCEPT OTHER PEOPLE WITHOUT RESERVATION

When we accept our own journey, it becomes easier to accept the journey of others.

If you are a wife, accept your partner.

Allow them to be who they are going to be.

Expecting someone to change to meet your needs will only frustrate you.

Acceptance is the highest form of love.

If you are a mother, many times your identity can revolve around your children.

We love our children so much and desire to give them the best life possible.

In desiring the best life for our children, we tend to project our own definition of an ideal life onto them.

We forget our children are individuals, and although we are entrusted to care and guide them as children, once they are adults they are ultimately responsible for themselves.

Some mothers grow so attached to their children that they get offended when they are not involved in their grown child's decision.

You raised your CHILD, now allow them to be an ADULT.

ACCEPTANCE

Attempting to over-involve yourself can damage a grown child's independence.

We would help our children tremendously if we allowed them to experience their own life.

Allow them to deal with their challenges on their own!

Too many parents want to get involved in their disagreements or issues at school.

If we continue to step in and attempt to save them from "hurts", then we won't allow them to grow as individuals.

Allow your children to maneuver through life's challenges so they can develop their own emotional fortitude.

Accept that life will throw many challenges at your children.

You can guide them and be a sounding board, but allow them to create solutions to their challenges and apply them as they see fit.

Furthermore, your children are not here to be your therapist or life partner.

The best thing you can do for your child is to be their mother, not their friend.

Of course, as they grow into adulthood this will change.

They will have their own issues in life.

Helping you maneuver through your adult challenges is not their responsibility.

Allow them to see you struggle while allowing them to see you create solutions for yourself.

They will learn through your actions.

Accept your role as a mother and show up as a guide for them in the most productive way possible.

It is OK for you to make mistakes, and for them to know you make them.

This helps them understand the journey of being human is not all pollyanna, "pie in the sky" happy.

Getting comfortable with being uncomfortable allows each of us to become emotionally and spiritually stronger.

Having kids can make us feel like we are getting another chance to do life "right".

Please remember your child is an individual and was not born so you could have another chance to live.

They came into this world for their own life experience.

Love doesn't bind or control.

Allow your child to evolve as the wonderful human being they are intended to become.

When they become an independent adult, they will appreciate your love and guidance.

You will have a strong and capable adult to be proud of.

Accepting others relieves so much pressure.

Exerting unnecessary pressure to control others can age you faster than you realize.

Be the observer of your life to truly age effectively.

Being an observer allows you to take the emotion out of participating in someone else's life.

ACCEPTANCE

If you are on a constant rollercoaster of emotion dictating the life of your family members, you will be exhausted.

This causes you to age way faster than needed.

EMBRACING THE DEATH OF YOUR PHYSICAL BODY

Death from this physical body is inevitable.

Not one of us will escape it.

Aging essentially brings us closer to this eventuality.

Tomorrow is not promised.

As you read this book, know there are many people who did not wake up today.

There are people who were tragically killed in accidents.

Life is a precious experience.

The more you appreciate the experience, the better your life will be.

> **Acceptance of death from this physical body allows you to fully appreciate life.**
>
> **Fully appreciating life allows you to be present in this moment.**
>
> **Being present in this moment allows you to age in the most effective way possible.**

Let's do a fun little thought experiment:

What if you could view each day as a gift?

A gift to "open" and appreciate.

It sounds cliché, but it doesn't make it any less true.

I seriously doubt you came into this existence to worry about each day, only to die on another one.

Worrying about how you will die - or when you will die - brings absolutely zero benefit to your life.

It actually depletes energy from your life source.

It causes worry lines to show up all over your face.

And if you truly desire to age productively, then what benefit does worrying have?

I have an 85 year old mentor, Betsy, who inspires me.

I recently took her to lunch and she informed me her twin sister had just passed away.

She said, "People keep asking me if I am OK.

I tell them I miss my sister tremendously, as we spoke every day.

I can not bring her back, but it's OK!

We had a pretty good run.

It does me no good to be sad all the time about it."

ACCEPTANCE

Betsy's attitude about life is to view every day as a gift.

She walks into a room and her light brightens the room at 100x magnification, even at 85 years of age.

Age does not define Betsy.

Besty's attitude and spirit define her.

An entire book could be written around the topic of death.

It is not my intention to convince you what death means or what is beyond death.

I view death as a transition.

I know I am more than my body.

I know at my core essence I am pure energy.

I won't simply disappear into a void upon exiting this body.

Explore what death means to you.

Tell yourself a story allowing you to add more productive life into your years.

Your beliefs around death will impact the quality of your life.

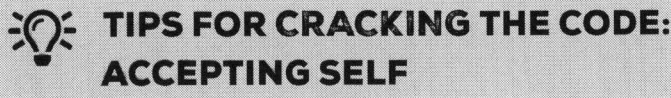

TIPS FOR CRACKING THE CODE: ACCEPTING SELF

1 - Practice mirror exercises

Sit in front of a mirror where you can look at yourself in the eyes.

Stare into them.

As you stare into your eyes, tell yourself something you would like to accept.

For example, if you don't believe you are beautiful or you mentally beat yourself up about it, then say out loud, "I am beautiful, I am beautiful."

You can add your name and emphasize it.

Say it until you can FEEL it.

See into your beautiful eyes beyond what you see with your eyes.

The best part about this exercise is when you get to the point where you can look into your eyes and say "I love you" and actually mean it.

This is a powerful exercise.

The more you practice, the more you beautifully express who you are.

It is a fun exercise when you are putting on your makeup or getting ready in the morning.

Play around with it and remind yourself how great it is to be you!

2 - Be kinder to yourself

When something does not go as you intended, STOP, PAUSE and BREATHE.

Remind yourself you are doing the best you can.

Ask yourself how you'd like to show up in this moment.

Do your best to stop saying thoughts to yourself like:
- *How can I be so stupid?*
- *I won't ever be able to look good.*
- *I wasn't meant to be happy.*
- *Life is meant to be hard for me.*
- *I have the worst luck*

Change the thoughts not allowing you to feel productive and fulfilled.

ACCEPTANCE

I remember when I was venturing into the self-improvement movement many years back.

I thought it was stupid to stop and tell myself anything.

If I had to act a certain way, then it was because I had to act a certain way.

I didn't want to keep policing my thoughts.

I felt like it wouldn't allow me to be present to the present moment.

As you become better at observing, you take out the emotional inclination to judge.

You simply notice a thought doesn't work for you.

Becoming the neutral observer in your own life is extremely empowering.

3 - Do things outside of your normal routine

When you can allow yourself to do different things in different ways, you realize there is so much more then your routine or schedule.

I have been the type to get stuck on schedules and deadlines.

This would cause me to get upset when things weren't going "my" way.

When you accept situations won't always turn out as intended, you will be more at peace.

4 - Start looking at your body with appreciation.

It is easy to look at our bodies as we age and start hating the way we look.

Instead, enjoy your body at all stages of your life.

Don't like your legs?

At least you have legs.

Don't like your hair?

Be thankful you have hair!

Getting more wrinkles?

LOVE each and every one of your wrinkles or pay for botox (depending on what feels best for you?)

This life experience brings so many opportunities for change and growth.

Each stage of your life will bring a new version of you to explore and love.

Stop worrying and start loving.

Your body is a beautiful vessel to carry you through this lifetime.

Treat it as such and enjoy the ride baby.

Accept yourself fully at any stage.

Accepting yourself doesn't mean you don't attempt to improve who you are.

I know I can always improve.

I accept where I am in my current journey, knowing I can continually get better.

5 - Practice going outside and interacting with others without makeup. Smile more and bring out your real essence.

As women, we often hide behind our makeup.

Many of us have been conditioned we must have makeup on to look good.

ACCEPTANCE

I have heard men say things like, "She still has to put on her war paint" or "My wife would not be caught dead in public without makeup".

I know makeup can "help" us look better (externally).

Sometimes we can use it as a crutch.

I recently went on a trip to Iceland with my brother and son.

I wore NO makeup on the whole trip.

When we got back and were at a family party, my brother said, "Wow Monica, you are wearing makeup.

You look good!"

Did I allow it to bother me?

No, because it is simply his opinion.

You will get opinions from other people.

Their opinion is just that: THEIR opinion.

You don't have to take ownership of other people's opinions!

It is OK to be comfortable with yourself, with or without makeup.

6 - Allow yourself to wear clothing that gives you a sense of sexiness or seductiveness.

Wear a sexy bra or underwear underneath your clothing.

It can allow you to tap into your vixen self.

As we age, we often lose our sex appeal because we believe we lose our value.

Explore your own femininity for you.

Your mate will find it sexy because you are exuding sexiness and seductiveness.

Wear something and feel sexy just because you can.

7 - Put on some music which can allow you to get your groove.

Close your eyes and feel the music.

Dance for you.

Touch yourself (not sexually rather seductively) and just move.

See and feel how this allows you to enjoy your body more.

8 - Notice something great about another woman and compliment her on it.

Genuinely pay attention to the beauty in others.

You will notice that the less critical you are of others, the less critical you are of yourself.

9 - STOP putting yourself down in front of others.

I have had women friends who continually put themselves down in the presence of others.

In some ways, it is a way to get a compliment back.

Putting yourself down does NOT benefit you.

As the saying goes, "If you don't have anything nice to say, then don't say anything at all."

This goes for you too.

If you don't have anything nice to say about yourself then don't say anything at all.

ACCEPTANCE

10 - When someone pays you a compliment, say "Thank You"

Receive a compliment.

It is ok to say "Thank you, I receive that".

You don't have to feel obligated to say something to return a compliment.

Fully receiving a compliment shows you fully accept yourself.

CHAPTER 2
EMBRACE YOUR INNER GODDESS

"You need not apologize for being brilliant, talented, gorgeous, rich or smart. Your success doesn't take away from anyone else's. It actually increases the possibility that others can have it too."

–Marianne Williamson

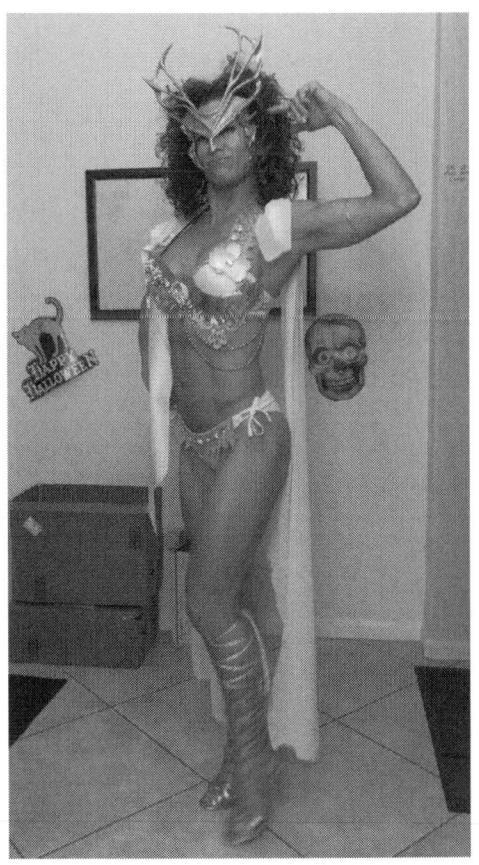

According to Google, the textbook definition of "goddess" is:
- *A female deity.*
- *A woman who is adored, especially for her beauty.*

Being a woman is beautiful.

It is a gift to be a woman.

But we are often told we are ugly, less than, too old, washed up... anything that isn't beautiful.

If anyone has ever told you that you are NOT beautiful, don't believe them.

It is a lie.

Don't believe the lies.

Is there a person or entity who has said you are not beautiful?

If so, I give you permission to dismiss and let go of their negative, sabotaging thoughts.

You are absolutely beautiful.

You don't think you are adored by anyone?

Adore yourself.

Allow yourself to be adored and know that you are worthy of being adored.

YES, KNOW YOU ARE ABSOLUTELY BEAUTIFUL!
FEEL THE BEAUTY.
BE BEAUTY.

All of this brings me to my main question: How do you view being a woman?

Do any of the thoughts below sound like something you may have thought or said about being a woman (or are thinking/saying right now)?

- *It is SUCH an inconvenience!*
- *I wish I was born a man!*
- *There is so much pressure to be beautiful, I hate wearing makeup.*
- *Because I'm a woman, my value decreases as I get older.*
- *As I get older, I get less attractive.*
- *I can't get pregnant; my body won't cooperate.*
- *I hate having my period.*
- *I hate going through menopause.*
- *My body gets destroyed from having children.*
- *The older I get, the less appreciated I am by others.*

We tell ourselves so many things about who we believe we are.

Who we wish we could be.

Or how inconvenient it is to be us right now.

But what if you could simply appreciate who you are without judgement?

There is only ONE you.

There will only be ONE you in all of history.

YOU are divinely created.

Even if you think you should have been a man, or prettier, or thinner or fatter,

When I was a young girl, I wished I was a boy.

I wanted my life to be easier.

I thought being a little boy would come with less problems.

I thought being a little boy would have other people appreciating me more.

Because I never fully appreciated being a girl, and wanting to be a little boy prevented me from enjoying the experience of being a little girl.

I certainly had some pain to go through to fully appreciate being a woman.

Fortunately, I now fully appreciate being a woman.

As women, it is so easy to point out all of our perceived flaws.

That's why it's so much more challenging to simply embrace our own beauty.

Why not be your own biggest fan instead?

I don't mean that in a stuck-up, conceited way.

What I mean is for you to embrace your beauty and LOVE it for what it is.

Not the beauty we have conditioned ourselves to believe.

We have been conditioned to believe and focus on our external beauty because this is what others see.

What about your beauty can you see?

Stop dismissing the awareness of your inner beauty; the beauty within.

Think about who/what feeds you the definition of 'beauty'.

The media (including social media), TV, others around you, and thousands of other people have taught us society's definition of beauty.

If we think about it, we recognize most of what we are taught about "beauty" is the collective masses perception of physical or 'external beauty'.

We are told that beauty is:

- Women who wear a bunch of makeup to cover up their "flaws"
- Filtered pictures to look better (Did you know there is even a term for people who look nothing like their pictures? My 15-year-old daughter taught me the term for a person who looks better in their pictures than in real life is called a 'catfish')
- A young woman with no wrinkles
- Wearing the latest fashion
- Hanging out with certain people

Why allow other people to determine what beauty means to you?

Allowing other people to determine your beauty will cause you to feel powerless.

This is why some women can get upset, as they dress to impress others.

Then when someone doesn't notice or pay attention to how they look, they become disappointed.

It does feel good to have others recognize and acknowledge our beauty.

But if we place our value on whether people notice us, we won't ever value ourselves.

Have you ever paid attention to what sells in the mainstream?

We have TV shows personalities discussing who wore the best outfit, who looks better, who is more famous, and so on.

Society teaches us to put other people on a pedestal while we sit back and "wish" our life could be better.

"If only I could…"

"Someday I'll be happier when XYZ happens" or "If I could only have enough money to buy ABC thing."

Despite these wishes, styles change continuously.

Fashion is constantly going through new trends while saying good-bye to old fads that were popular just a few months/years ago.

There are times I don't want to give away old clothes because I know it will come back in fashion again.

I now see my daughter wearing styles I thought were hip in my high school days.

People and opinions change all the time.

Continually attempting to please society is extremely imprudent as society is always undergoing some major shift or change.

In a sense, society as a whole will never be truly happy.

Therefore, why would you allow society to dictate what can make you be or feel happy?

Are you participating in society's view of what beauty is, or what the word "beauty" means?

Do you think you can only be beautiful with makeup on?

Do you think you have to get manicured nails and hair in order to be beautiful?

In my personal worldview I know God does NOT make mistakes.

I know that my inner and outer beauty are independent of whatever propaganda society tries to force-feed me.

YOU were given the gift of being born a female.

THIS IS BEAUTIFUL.

Why resist who you are?

There are many factors and influences that can change the course of one's life.

These range from what is fed emotionally to you while in the womb, all the way to how you are raised (i.e. what you are fed mentally and emotionally as you grow up).

We also have our childhood environment, which affects who we become as adults.

The way you have viewed circumstances in your life will dictate how you allow yourself to show up.

These same circumstances determine if you are in full appreciation of being a woman.

Most of us did not have a perfect childhood.

I know for sure that my childhood was anything but perfect.

I wasn't raised to appreciate who I was.

I was raised to survive.

My mom had 4 children within 3 years and my dad left within 3 weeks of my little brother being born.

We struggled.

My mom didn't have time to manage all 4 of us and work full time.

I became a tomboy.

I hated dresses.

I was awkward and hated being me.

I felt like I was being punished for being born into my skin.

My mind seemed to be my own worst enemy.

I would pray for God to turn off my mind.

It seemed to 'talk down' to me all day and night.

We all have a past, and for some the past is not great.

Why would you allow your past to dictate who you are today?

So many of us are adults walking around with the mentality of kids holding onto ideals fed to us as children.

We have physically grown up but are still making decisions based on our inner child protecting us from being hurt again.

The irony is that protecting ourselves causes us to not fully participate in life.

We build "walls" because the pain hurts so bad.

We don't ever want to feel that pain again.

It takes doing the internal work to move beyond the pain of your past.

This can be done through therapy with a professional, through self-introspection in silence, taking self-improvement classes - the options available to you right now are virtually endless.

Unfortunately, many people refuse to deal with the pain they feel inside.

For these people, living in survival mode protects them from the danger of the unknown.

It becomes a familiar pattern they are at ease with.

Why would they bother breaking this pattern, knowing that it will be a difficult and arduous path?

If this describes you right now, you are living in your own mental prison.

Believe me when I say I have been where you are.

I know from first-hand experience how difficult it can appear to even consider change.

There is SO much more to YOU, then how you have been conditioned.

Why not get comfortable with pain?

If you get comfortable with pain, then you won't resist getting hurt.

When you don't resist getting hurt, then you show up in life as your authentic self.

Showing up in life as your authentic self allows more of your true goddess to shine.

It's like my personal mentor Matthew Ferry once told me:

"What you resist, persists. What you accept, transforms."

I know I used this quote in the previous chapter and it is SO important to take in.

Once you do, it transforms your ability to embrace your inner femininity.

WHAT STORY WILL YOU CHOOSE TO TELL YOURSELF TODAY?

Have you ever felt there is more to you than you are sharing with the world?

GOOD NEWS!

Your intuition is exactly right, and that's because there IS more to you than you realize.

The goddess inside you wants to break free.

I would like you to read these words, close your eyes and FEEL them.

Start to notice yourself believing in these words more and more with each repetition.

Make it a daily habit to repeat these affirmative words with full faith and conviction when you look at yourself in the mirror:

I AM BEAUTIFUL.
I AM DIVINELY CREATED.
I AM WORTHY OF AN AMAZING LIFE.
I AM A GODDESS FULLY EXPRESSED.

The rest of what you tell yourself is simply a story.

You can say those words are "just a story" too.

But what story do you think is more productive:

The story where you build yourself up, or the story where you unfairly tear yourself down?

If you're telling yourself a negative story, you may end up saying things like:

- "I am not beautiful."
- "I won't ever be able to find someone to love."
- "I won't ever find someone to love me."
- "I am not worthy."
- "I always make mistakes."
- "I am meant to work at this job for the rest of my life."
- "I don't have a great body."

With liberalism and feminism, the beauty of being a woman can get lost.

We attempt to protect and fight for what is already inherently ours.

We think we have to compete with men to prove we have more talents or as much value as they do.

Instead of competing, what if we cooperated with one another?

There is more power in unity than division.

Competition only creates division.

Working together creates a sense of unity.

A man is not better than a woman.

A woman is not better than a man.

We are all human beings.

Each one of us has our own journey.

This journey of being human can be rewarding for our species when we stop competing with one another.

We don't have anything to prove to anyone.

"Fighting" and "attacking" other people because we aren't respected is not productive for anyone.

The anger inside of you wanting to hurt someone else takes away your beauty.

Dr. Martin Luther King, Jr stated so eloquently,

> *"Darkness can not drive out darkness, only light can do that; hate can not drive out hate, only love can do that."*

And he's exactly right.

After all, how can your true goddess power shine when you are attacking others?

Sadly, we live in times where many women are looking at what they don't like and what they should complain about before accepting anything.

If we are continually looking for what isn't working in our life, how can we expand the beauty inside of ourselves?

Beauty doesn't expand by looking at what is ugly.

Beauty expands by seeing the beauty already there and expanding upon it.

I am not speaking about equal rights, or how someone else 'should' treat a woman (All people should be respected).

I am speaking to YOU, the woman reading this book.

You are beautifully created.

You are a goddess fully expressed.

You were created as a woman.

You have the capacity to grow another life inside you.

Your body changes SO much throughout your lifetime.

There is TRUE beauty in that.

Do I mean you are only beautiful if you have a child?

NO.

I am saying your body was made to produce and nurture life.

This is fantastically amazing.

In today's day and age, it's far too easy to take for granted our power as women.

I am not speaking of power as in force.

I am speaking about power from presence and BEING.

Being a woman comes with wisdom when one listens to her heart and trusts her own inner guidance.

It is easy to mistake "inner guidance" with mental chatter in our head.

We go by our emotions in the moment (mad, sad, angry, anxious, etc.).

We confuse them as true feelings and then act without truly knowing the source of our thoughts.

But KNOWING is just that: KNOWING!

When you practice knowing what is best for you, you practice using your GODDESS power.

When you act off of your knowing and with steps of faith, all turns out for the greater good.

When it doesn't turn out as you thought, please realize something better lays beyond.

You don't allow circumstances to dictate your worth.

As your wonderful goddess self, practice trusting you before anyone else.

Don't believe me, or your mother, or your children.

TRUST "you" so you can KNOW your beautiful goddess power.

Feel it radiating out into the world.

A true goddess blesses herself and others by BEING beauty.

Stop looking at beauty from an external perspective.

This is causing you to age and it distracts you from enjoying the process.

Your external package will always be in a state of change.

Focus on who you are becoming, and how you are sharing it with the world.

A true goddess is willing to be honest about who she is and what she is allowing into her life.

Look at situations in your life as feedback.

If you are continually dealing with people who disrespect you, ask yourself where you may be disrespecting others or yourself.

There is no need to beat yourself up by allowing guilt to take over.

It takes courage to truly love and accept yourself, knowing you are evolving into an even better version.

It is easy to come home, flop in front of the television and "disappear" for 3 hours to watch your favorite shows.

But it takes courage to review your day/week and see where you can improve.

It takes courage to take responsibility for your life and how it is evolving (positive or negative).

It takes courage to respect your body and exercise.

It takes courage to know your body is a temple, and feed it nourishing foods.

It takes courage to stand in your Goddess power and SHINE!

EMBRACING YOUR DIVINE FEMININE AND MASCULINE AS YOUR GODDESS SELF

Right now, we seem to have a spotlight on the "Divine Feminine" as if this is the best way to be a woman.

Men and women both have masculine and feminine energy.

When there is flow with our masculine and feminine nature, we show up more powerfully.

Embrace all aspects of your being.

As a woman, when you reject some of your femininity, you show up more masculine (man-like).

There is nothing wrong with being a woman, just as there is nothing wrong with being a man.

Embrace your whole divine essence.

Ignore what society says, because society is miserable.

Modern-day society chooses to look at what can offend us, rather than what can enrich us.

Love who you are.

Some people think changing their sex will make them feel better.

But it will never change how YOU feel about yourself.

You still see with the same eyes and feel the same emotions as before.

But here's the thing: You are FAR MORE than a sexual being.

You have value because of who you are, NOT because of your sexual preference.

Sexual preference is only a small segment of who you are.

When a woman allows her masculinity to dominate, it becomes increasingly tough to find a masculine man.

Quite often, like repels like, and opposites attract.

Whether you are in a heterosexual or homosexual relationship, there is always a masculine and a feminine identity.

So if you are a woman and desire to be with a man, then realize that as a masculine woman, you will only attract a feminine man.

Understanding your feminine and masculine power will allow you to direct your goddess power more effectively, and in a positive and healthy way.

Know the beautiful dance between your own masculine and feminine energy.

Observe how you maneuver through situations in your life, then assess what works for you.

If you become dominant during stress, do you feel good about how you show up to others?

If not, how can you shift?

If you are with a more masculine man and you have issues complying with his requests (this does not mean complying with his demands), ask yourself where your issues come from.

Are you OK leading, or do you want to lead?

If you have challenges allowing others to lead, why don't you trust others?

Your life will continually give you feedback by the results you attain.

If you are not happy with how your life is evolving, change it.

By getting in touch with your goddess self, you give yourself power to see with eyes of love.

This allows you to take action and create positive change in your life.

No one can fill a void for you.

If you are feeling less than, or out of touch with your femininity, start exploring what you can do for yourself from an emotional perspective.

HOW TO BE A SEXUAL GODDESS, NO MATTER YOUR AGE

You can be a sexual goddess at any point in your life.

It begins with an internal beingness.

Many of us are taught to restrict ourselves when it comes to sex or sexuality.

We hold back for various reasons (conditioning, insecurity, past traumas, etc.).

Please understand that much of our conditioning surrounding sex is what society (and oftentimes religion) has made up.

When you let go of what your mind identifies as sex, you feel free to express who you really are with your mate or for yourself.

Being a sexual goddess isn't just about the act itself.

It is about being in touch with who you are as a woman.

It is knowing you can be sensual in any interaction without being obtrusive.

It is knowing you can lay down and touch your body with love and appreciation.

Sensuality can be caressing your mate, giving soft kissing, and genuine embraces.

Being a sexual goddess can also mean showing up as a vixen to your mate.

But it doesn't have to be every time either.

The more you become in tune with who you are, the less necessary sex becomes.

Sex becomes more of a way to share your beingness.

When you come from this perspective, the exchange between you and your partner is more authentic.

There is less stress or angst.

Less proving.

In being a sexual goddess, you realize you are not limited to only being a sexual goddess.

You know your goddess self can be any type of goddess, and at the time of your choosing.

When you can fully express your true goddess self, you become fully versatile.

You learn to express a specific type of goddess at any given moment.

Let me explain what I mean by being a different type of goddess.

You may want to be a healing goddess, nurturing and attending to a loved one who is sick.

You may go home to your husband who has set up a nice meal for the two of you.

In the evening, you can step outside or go to another room, close your eyes and visually release the healing goddess to welcome the sexual goddess.

The sexual goddess can bring sensuality to the moment, caressing her partner and sharing in beautiful intimacy.

As women, we have the power to take on many roles in any given day.

I love "role playing".

I play silly games with myself all the time.

If my husband and I are going out to dance, then I "put on" my youthful dancing self.

If I am in business mode, then I "put on" my "badass business" goddess self.

It's so fun wearing different identities!

At times before my husband and I are intimate, I envision myself as the sexual goddess I desire to be.

I close my eyes and step into her.

I allow myself to feel and see what it would be like to be her.

This makes our intimate time fun and enjoyable for both us.

It keeps my husband guessing as to which goddess will come through:

The sensual seductress or the freaky "bus stop" goddess.

Be open to your sexual goddess coming through!

Be open to your sensuality coming through, no matter your age.

This doesn't mean simply limiting yourself to expressing your sexuality/sensuality with your husband/mate.

As we age, we have a tendency to lose respect for our bodies.

We don't touch ourselves with love or sensuality.

I am not referring to masturbation.

I am referring to being kind to our bodies.

Loving our bodies as it goes through change over time.

Women develop a destructive tendency to mentally beat themselves up because they don't look a certain way.

It gets worse as we get older because it's harder to even look at ourselves naked!

Therefore, love every ounce of you no matter how 'bad' you think you are aging.

This is your body, your vehicle/vessel.

You are a true goddess, so treat yourself as such.

See your whole self as the beautiful being you are, regardless of how old and/or saggy you appear.

Respect your body as it goes through changes.

It is one thing to love and accept yourself, and another thing altogether to destroy your body by eating foods you know won't help you.

Destroying your body is not an act of self-love.

Allowing yourself to become overweight, not exercising and drinking alcohol is not showing self-love.

You are actually hurting yourself and ensuring you die sooner rather than later.

Our bodies are temples.

When treated with respect, self-care, and love, our temples radiate light.

When you can allow yourself to be mentally and physically free during intimacy, it allows for a pleasurable experience for you and your partner.

There is nothing sexier than a partner who is free, confident and willing to explore with one another.

Being in touch with your sexual goddess opens the door to a deeper intimacy with your mate and yourself.

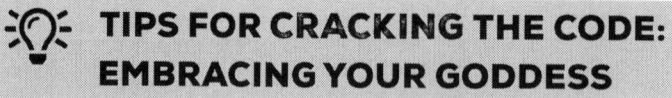

TIPS FOR CRACKING THE CODE: EMBRACING YOUR GODDESS

1 - As you get ready, show appreciation for each part of your body.

As you apply lotion or soap to your skin, thank your skin for doing its job.

Tell your arm and/or body how much you appreciate and love it.

Look at your skin and love it (age spots and all).

Talk to yourself about how you love being you.

This may feel weird at first, especially if your tendency has been to beat yourself up for all your flaws.

Keep practicing, it will get easier over time.

If you feel comfortable, speak the positive affirmations in this chapter to your body out loud.

Before you know it, you will believe your love-affirming thoughts, and your skin will feel and look better.

Remember: Our skin is made up of cells and what you feed it - thoughts, foods, skin care products - determine its appearance.

Special Note My husband Jay Campbell and his business partner Nick Andrews have created a specialized skin care company (Aesir) which sells peptide cosmetic formulations that dramatically improve skin quality as one ages.

I have been regularly using their products now since the beginnings of this year and the results I have at nearly 48 years young are astonishing.

Here's some more information about these products…

> Aging is fundamentally a breakdown of cellular life processes leading to wear and tear over time.
>
> With current technology at our disposal, we can slow down the accumulation of wear and tear at the cellular level, and to some degree reverse it.
>
> Diet and exercise, as well as various supplements play a huge role.
>
> But there are proactive steps we can take in the form of skin care.

Welcome to the world of peptides.

Small amino acid chains (i.e. peptides) have been around since the 60's.

These amino acid chains can act as signaling molecules directly, profoundly affecting the behavior of biological systems at the cellular level.

Many peptides are very fragile and are only useful in most cases as SubQ (subcutaneous) injections.

There are a handful of peptides which have been proven through extensive clinical research to be effective topically (as a transdermal cream).

Utilizing these topically-effective peptides can allow you to turn back your aging clock.

GHK-CU is a small peptide that has proven itself highly effective.

In the case of GHK-CU, topical use through a serum or face cream thickens the dermis, tightens loose skin and improves elasticity.

It also improves skin density and firmness while reducing fine lines and deep wrinkles.

It can also dramatically improve skin clarity, while reducing photodamage and mottled hyper-pigmentation via increasing keratinocyte proliferation.

As fantastic as all that scientific terminology sounds, the "everything but the kitchen sink" description is backed up by decades of clinical research, including benefits beyond what are listed here.

Peptides are truly powerful molecules and the inevitable future of optimization medicine.

They are able to interact with their target areas at the cellular and genetic level.

This provides peptides with the ability to deliver results far beyond many other skin care approaches.

However, it is important to remember these changes don't happen overnight.

Some people see noticeable changes quickly, while others may take weeks before changes are noticeable.

It is now entirely possible to go far beyond maintaining moisture for your skin as you age.

With the smart usage of specific peptide based cosmetic formulations, you can aid your body in slowing and/or reversing its aging clock.

2 - As you put your makeup on in the morning, remind yourself how beautiful you are.

See yourself through the eyes of your inner child (accepting, and with eyes of love).

If you notice more wrinkles, or the bags under your eyes seem bigger than usual, energetically send love to these areas.

Be softer with yourself.

When your mind keeps pointing out your flaws, remind yourself how beautiful you are.

Think of yourself as an infant learning self-worth all over again.

This time, you will be teaching your inner child how to stop relying on outside sources for validation.

3 - Visualize yourself as the goddess you know you are.

When I have moments of insecurity (it can pop up for any of us, and at any time), I close my eyes and picture myself on the top of a mountain with a white, flowy dress.

My hands are outstretched, my hair is blowing in the wind and I feel myself being the goddess I know I am.

I feel the freedom in this feeling.

I smile, and at times a tear comes to my eye.

I mentally step into my inner goddess and KNOW she is there with me.

This is powerful because it allows us to know there is more to reality than our experience of the external world.

4 - Put reminders in your phone (or on your calendar) to pop up at different points throughout the day.

Type the reminders in your phone as a way to inspire you.

If having "I love you goddess" pop up in the afternoon gets you inspired, then write those words down.

I have all kinds of sayings in my phone to remind me of my own inner strength.

5 - Journal about your journey.

Ask yourself productive questions to ignite your power, such as:
- *How can I contribute to others?*
- *Am I being the best version of myself now?*
- *What can I do to improve the quality of my life and those I love?*
- *Are you being your best goddess self?*

Once you ask your questions, answer them with complete honesty.

See what comes to you.

Through practice, you will get to know yourself more and more.

It's a fun way to explore who you are!

6 - Send blessings to other people.

Since you are a goddess, then naturally you would want to bless others.

Share your goddess powers, and ignite them by being a blessing to all.

Close your eyes and say a small prayer for someone.

Surround them in light and see them with eyes of love.

CHAPTER 3
LOVE FULLY

"Love is like the wind, you can't see it but you can feel it."
-Nicholas Sparks

Have you ever felt fully loved?

Have you ever loved anyone (including yourself) fully?

To love and be loved is one of the greatest experiences we can share in life.

Authentic love is one of the greatest lessons to learn while in this physical experience.

If you have a child, do you remember what it was like to hold your child for the first time?

This was when I felt this authentic love fully for the first time.

This little being came from inside of me.

I housed this baby in my body for 9 months.

Once I got to hold this precious child in my arms, a rush of emotion came over me and I instantly knew the feeling of pure love.

From this experience, I opened up to the journey and exploration of self-love.

Unfortunately, many women go through this same experience, but quickly lose touch with their own ability to love themselves and others.

I'm no exception, because I was thrown off the journey of self-love as quickly as I started it.

So what happens?

Why do we become so unloving?

Life takes over.

We get hurt.

We feel used.

We feel worn out.

We forget how to love and be loved.

As a result, we can hold conditions for our love, love for ourselves and love for others.

Think about the conditions you hold in regards to your love for others?

Are they productive or unproductive?

See if any of these examples resonate with you.

I can only love you if:

- *You remember my birthday.*
- *You treat me how I want to be treated.*
- *You put the toothpaste cap back on.*
- *You tell me I look good.*
- *You treat me like your queen.*
- *You take me out to dinner 2 times a week.*
- *You take me on trips.*
- *You speak highly about me to others.*

Think about how many conditions you have about loving YOURSELF.

Are they productive or unproductive?

See if you can relate with any of the following examples.

I only love myself when:

- *I eat the right foods.*
- *I do what I say.*
- *I have the "right" friends.*
- *I go to the gym.*
- *I don't eat the wrong foods.*
- *I am wearing the right outfit.*
- *I am with the right mate.*
- *I look good.*

If your conditions for loving others and yourself are unproductive, why do you set such conditions (Remember, you get to decide what is productive or unproductive)?

Why intentionally make the act of love much more difficult than it has to be?

Conditional love restricts, while authentic love frees.

Loving fully allows you to truly live.

Truly living allows you to age more effectively.

In my eyes, we are love.

Unfortunately, our environment and our experiences can take over and mask our ability to love.

This often disguises our true identity.

We allow situations, conditioning, various circumstances and beliefs to dictate our ability to love and be loved.

WHAT "LANGUAGE OF LOVE" ARE YOU SPEAKING TO YOURSELF AND OTHERS?

I love Gary Chapman's book The 5 Love Languages and how he explains the way we give and receive love.

If you haven't read his book, it is a must read!

According to Chapman, we give love in the way we FEEL loved.

When we aren't feeling loved, it can be because someone we care about isn't speaking our 'love language'.

The 5 Love Languages are:
1. *Words of Affirmation*
2. *Physical Touch*
3. *Receiving Gifts*
4. *Quality Time*
5. *Acts of Service*

For me, I feel the most love with "Acts of Service".

When people do things for me, I feel important and significant.

Throughout my life, I have always done things for people.

If something had to be done, I did it because I wanted people to know I cared.

It's funny how I've loved people as I've felt loved: By doing.

Even in times of stress, I love myself by doing something productive.

Whether I work out, go for a walk, get a pedicure, I am doing something to feel loved.

On top of acting in accordance with respect to other people's love languages, it's equally important to make sure you are speaking your own love language.

The best way to love fully is to begin by loving yourself fully.

This makes loving others so much more fun.

Taking a look at your own life: Are you loving as you feel loved or loving as others feel loved?

Let's be clear: Loving fully does not mean worrying.

Worrying is fear based. Love is LOVE.

When I was a new mom, my mom would continually tell me "Monica, I worry because I care. When you care, you worry."

Because of this training, I thought I had to worry about my family and children because this would show them how much I loved them.

Little did I realize that this nonstop worrying only depleted my energy.

Not only did worrying rob me of my personal power, but I surrounded my children and loved ones in fear.

I never want my family or children to be surrounded in fear,

I want them to feel and be strengthened in love.

Love strengthens.

Fear depletes.

If you truly desire to age effectively, then love fully.

Love because you are a full expression of love.

HOW TO FINALLY START LOVING YOURSELF, OTHERS AND LIFE AGAIN

Do you think you don't know how to love?

Well, here's the good news: YOU'RE WRONG!

You DO know how to love.

You just simply forgot over time and need to remind yourself.

Start by being kind.

Be kind to yourself and others.

Not because you expect something back.

But because you simply desire to be kind.

See how that makes you feel.

When you are kind without expectations, it opens the door to love.

As a child, do you recall the grandparents or teachers you felt most loved by?

They seemed to have a beautiful presence to them.

This is because they loved without barriers.

You felt accepted by them.

Loving others not only helps you, but it also helps others.

Loving fully begins by how your brain define things.

When you are outside, do you focus on the things you don't like about the environment?

Or are you appreciating the beauty of a flower, or perhaps the gentle sound of a water fountain?

Let me be clear: Love doesn't mean you are ignorant to the dangers in life.

It doesn't mean you allow strangers into your life without placing care and consideration for you and your family.

It doesn't mean you allow people to walk all over you.

Love is also not misplaced aggression.

Some people are passionate about animals and want to protest against the abuse of animals.

In their protest, they begin to destroy other people's property and "hate" on their way of being.

As sad as it is that anyone could abuse an animal, fighting them with hate won't ever stop the process or help you.

Fighting them with hate is essentially bringing you to the same energetic level as the abuser of animals.

I hear people say time and time again how much better our world would be with peace.

Peace begins with love.

There is no way to heal hatred with more hatred.

Heal hatred with love.

It starts from you and extends outward.

If you are gonna age more effectively, living in a more loving world will only help.

💡 TIPS FOR CRACKING THE CODE: LOVING FULLY

1 - Show yourself love by respecting yourself.

If you have a vice, how can you move beyond it?

Are you smoking?

Don't smoke for a day, or 2 or 3.

See how long you can go before you pick up a cigarette.

Give yourself evidence you respect yourself more.

Make this a fun game for yourself.

This is not about beating yourself up if you don't follow through.

If you allow yourself to overeat or eat foods you know don't help your body, then start by eating less of the crappy food.

2 - Pamper yourself from time to time.

When was the last time you got a massage?

When was the last time you got a pedicure or manicure?

Allow yourself some time to be pampered.

3 - Send love jolts.

From time to time, I will send a text to someone I haven't spoken to in a while and let them know I am sending them a "love jolt".

What is this?

It can be anything; an old pic of us that feels loving, or something I love about them.

It is a way for me to give them evidence of how much they mean to me.

4 - Smile more often.

Smiling helps you feel better, and it makes it easier to love while smiling.

5 - As you go to sleep at night, surround those you care about with love.

You can stretch it out over the world too.

We are all energy.

Love is an energy.

If we are all energy and energy travels, direct the energy to where you would like it to go.

6 - Send love to those who irritate you.

I have done this with my ex-husband because he has upset me many times.

I have felt used and disrespected by him, too many times to count.

When I focus on how much (I feel) he has done to me, I can get really emotional or sad.

If I allow myself to move away from the pain, I send him love because I cannot control how he will ever be.

He is his own person.

I divorced him for a reason.

All I can control is what I send out to him.

I would rather have love coming from me then hatred.

It feels so much more enriching.

7 - When you find yourself worrying about someone or something, turn your worry to love.

When my children began getting older and becoming more independent, my mind attempted to scare me about all the horrible possibilities that could happen out in the world.

At night, it was the worst.

I would lay awake at night thinking about what could happen if they had not gotten home yet.

So many horrible scenarios would play out in my mind.

This feels horrible to me, and I can imagine the energy I am sending to them while being in fear and thinking about them.

One night, I realized I was hurting myself and them by doing this.

I stopped and said to myself, "Instead of sending them fear, worry and doubt, what if I simply send them love and protection?"

Now, when my mind attempts to scare me, I surround the situation and/or person in the energy of love.

I will do this with a color that comes to mind.

I surround the person or situation with this color, and picture them enclosed in a bubble of protection energy with this energy and color.

Knowing I am surrounding them in protection and love eases my mind.

I know it also helps the person or situation I am concerned about.

I can tell you it FEELS much better to send LOVE then to send fear.

CHAPTER 4
LOOK FOR EVIDENCE

"What you think you become. What you feel you attract. What you imagine you create."
–Buddha

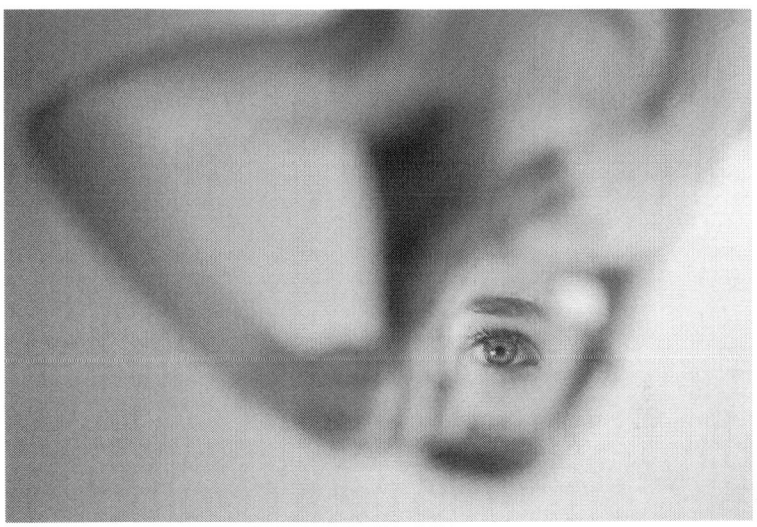

When you are in public, look around you:

What do you see?

- Do you see any older people who are weak and frail? Looking at them, what comes to mind?
- When you watch a movie, how are older people portrayed? When you see them, what comes to your mind?
- How did your mom and grandma age? What comes to your mind when you think about the way they aged?

We are constantly surrounded by plenty of evidence to indicate that getting older SUCKS!

We see people in wheelchairs, walking hunched back, wrinkles everywhere, cranky all the time, and dependent on others.

We participate in the 'sick" care medical system, bombarded by TV and radio with messages on how to 'fight' sickness to deal with the effects of aging.

We are fed with nonstop negativity about aging.

There are perspectives of weakness and victimhood coming from every direction.

Let me ask you this:

If you have women in your life who are older and living kickass lives, what do you tell yourself about them?

Do you use them as a source of inspiration?

Or as another excuse as to why you can not be better?

Our mind is the ultimate critic and judge.

Our mind will condition us to think aging breaks us down.

Did you realize what we see with our eyes is due to our brain?[1]

If our brain is feeding us the information for our eyes to see, then the following holds true:

If you are visually feeding yourself evidence of frailty and sickness, this is how you will see life as you age.

---

[1] https://nei.nih.gov/healthyeyes/howwesee

HOW TO STOP RELYING ON THE "SICK CARE MEDICAL SYSTEM" AND START TAKING CONTROL OF YOUR HEALTH

In today's society, we are all about "quick fixes".

Are you sick or can't do something?

In the "sick care" medical system, the solution is:

"Here, take a pill. It will help you get better. And by the way, there are only several potential side effects that can cause pain, discomfort or maybe even death."

The current way of dealing with sickness and aging in today's society is causing us to become frailer.

We are losing touch with our own personal power.

Part of the "sick care" medical care system involves continually looking and paying attention to your family history.

But being so in tune with your family history can actually be a sick diagnosis for you.

Don't get the wrong idea: Your family history can be an effective way to diagnose illness.

However, way too many men and women are using it as a crutch and a cop-out.

"My mom died of breast cancer, so I am more likely to get breast cancer by the time I am 35 years old."

This perspective can cause you to hyper-focus on your breasts and become paranoid every time you feel something is "off" with them.

I have lost count of how many times I have heard women say, "This sickness runs in my family, so there's nothing I can do about it".

Can you imagine continually feeding yourself this information?

Why would you keep saying this to yourself, knowing it puts you in a constant state of protection?

Again, let's be clear...

- Am I saying not to take care of yourself? NO!
- Am I saying not to pay attention to any issues that arise as you age? NOPE!
- Am I saying not to listen to the doctor you trust? ABSOLUTELY NOT!

I am saying you are YOU.

Your mom is your mom.

Your aunt is your aunt.

Your grandmother is your grandmother.

We are all different.

As my husband has become very fond of saying, every single human being on the planet is biochemically unique.

You have no idea what was going on in your loved one's life, or what they were exposed to when they acquired their illness.

It could have been from lifestyle factors such as an unhealthy diet, lack of exercise and/or poor stress management

Knowing this, why would you choose to be attached to their sickness?

There is a higher risk for any of us to have a sickness because someone in our family had it previously.

There is an even higher risk for you to contract the same illness, especially if you continually tell yourself you have a higher chance of getting the same sickness.

What if you could make some healthy lifestyle changes, rather than continually telling yourself you are prone to get the same sickness/disease?

Feed yourself with messages of wholeness, peace, and love.

For example: *"I am a perfect body of health, fully enjoying this life experience."*

Do you think that sounds better than continually telling yourself *"Breast cancer runs in my family, so I have an increased chance of getting breast cancer"*?

I think the answer is obvious.

Ultimately, the choice is yours.

It takes serious inner work to recondition yourself with the belief you are your own individual person, regardless of your family history.

You can detach from the information given to you about how certain things are carried down generation after generation.

Am I saying this will 100% deter you from NOT getting cancer or other genetically predisposed diseases?

NO.

I am saying to give yourself a different perspective to strengthen your body and mind.

If giving yourself more love by building yourself up (instead of tearing yourself down) and appreciating yourself gives you a better quality of life, why not give yourself the gift without expecting a certain outcome?

Expecting to NEVER get a disease can cause you to breakdown further, if you were ever to contract one.

For this reason alone, acceptance of who you are is crucial.

In doing so, you will know you can handle anything that comes your way.

Use the information of your family history as a way to strengthen yourself.

If you are told you are more prone to getting breast cancer, receive but don't accept it.

In this situation, appreciation can be expressed by giving your breasts more love.

Touch and fondle your breasts.

Send them love energetically.

Have your lover tenderly touch your breasts and suck your nipples.

Enjoy your breasts.

So many women want to protect themselves end up depriving themselves of love.

Each part of our body has cell memory[2].

It is important to send love to each and every one of your cells.

Your brain, your heart, your throat, your stomach, your fingers, your toes – anything you can think of.

Scan your body internally and see (or FEEL) what areas of your body may want and/or need a bit of extra love.

Loving yourself doesn't mean abusing yourself.

---

2 https://naturalhealthcourses.com/2015/06/cellular-memory-and-how-it-works/

LOOK FOR EVIDENCE

Thinking your stomach needs more love doesn't mean eating a gallon of ice cream will give it to you.

Close your eyes and thank your stomach for doing its job, surround it in white (or a color you choose) light.

Use common sense.

Remember: You are living in your body. Know what is best for you.

STOP "LOOKING" FOR EVIDENCE OF DISEASE. INSTEAD, SEEK OUT EVIDENCE OF HEALTH

Here's an all-too-common example of how women focus on finding evidence for having a certain disease...

Say you grow up in a family where 3 generations have died of breast cancer.

Your belief is that you will die of breast cancer.

You become obsessed with whether or not you have breast cancer.

You get your mammogram once a year, do self-examinations, donate to breast cancer awareness, and wear pink bows to show your support against fighting breast cancer.

Whether you realize it or not, your focus is all around 'breast cancer'.

It doesn't matter whether you want to fight or prevent breast cancer because your whole being is centered around breast cancer.

Because of this nonstop thinking, you are far more likely to develop breast cancer.

This doesn't mean you will die of breast cancer, but there's a greater chance you will develop breast cancer.

Afterall, your being KNOWS breast cancer and the energy around breast cancer more than anything else.

Breast Cancer Awareness Month is a great cause, but we are focusing on 'Breast Cancer'.

What if we made it "Healing Month" instead?

Rather than spread pink ribbons everywhere so people could focus on cancer, we would spread these ribbons to focus on healing.

Sure, this may hinder the funds 'Breast Cancer Research' accumulates, but is this month truly about the money for research, or about becoming/being healthy?

Here's a shockingly common occurrence: Ever known researchers who develop a disease because they are looking for cures?

Some become so immersed in their research, they end up contracting the disease.

I recall hearing a story about a woman who would tell her children she would develop breast cancer one day, all while holding her hand over her right breast.

She eventually contracted breast cancer over her right breast, which ultimately caused her death.

Keep looking at your family history with despair and concern, and you are likely to have the disease show up (After all, it's what you have spent all your time and energy preparing for).

Life works in a similar fashion: The more evidence you give a "truth", the more you bring your truth to the surface.

TAKE TOTAL AND COMPLETE CONTROL OF YOUR OWN HEALTH

We have been trained to be "concerned" if a loved one died of cancer, or had a life-threatening illness.

We are then told we have an increased chance of acquiring the same sickness.

Ironically, you are more likely to have the same sickness by having the same habits as your loved one acquired (worrying, poor diet, lack of exercise, chronic stress, etc.), rather than simply being related to them.

Experiment with this yourself.

Challenge yourself to see yourself as an individual who is healthy, whole and complete.

Now, I know what you may be thinking:

"Give me evidence about your theory! I want scientific studies to prove what you are saying!"

Create your own study instead!

Be your own ongoing experiment.

Why wait for someone else to set up conditions for their own study when NO study will have your exact conditions or circumstances?

This is your life.

Give yourself permission to be the scientist of your own health.

Again, I am not a doctor.

I am not here to diagnose you.

I am here to give you a different perspective.

What you do with it is up to you.

Everything I'm sharing with you in this book is what I know to be true for me.

I have done all the things I'm advising you to do with my own health.

I don't compare myself to other people in my family and focus on what illnesses they have.

You may think *"Oh no, how can you be so dumb?"*, but frankly that does not concern me.

This is my life journey, and I choose to live it as productively as possible.

I tell myself every day, "I am a perfect body of health".

I know and feel this in my heart and my soul.

Does this 100% guarantee I won't get a sickness? No.

Yet, I am happier living my life.

I enjoy today because I am not promised tomorrow.

I could die in a car crash, so why do I need to continually stress myself out about acquiring a disease?

I know I will die one day, and no matter how it happens, I am ready.

I am not a doctor, nor do I pretend to be one, so feel free to doubt all I say.

But here's what I do know.

I am a woman who lives a kick-ass life based on my terms.

I rarely go to the doctor.

LOOK FOR EVIDENCE

Would you rather follow a doctor (who is often out of shape themselves), or KNOW yourself better so you can decide what is truly best for you?

Remember: Doctors are trained to follow a procedure when dealing with patients.

The procedure is "family history" and "prescription medication".

As a result, we have ingrained beliefs associated with our family history.

When it comes to your well-being, it is important to question how things are done and whether they are in your best interest.

If you feel like your doctor has your best interests in mind, then by all means listen to them.

There are great doctors and there are crappy doctors.

If there is something you don't agree with regarding your doctor's opinion, voice your concern or switch doctors.

I cannot emphasize this enough: Doctors are human beings and can make mistakes.

Do not put them on a pedestal and believe they are "ALL knowing".

Yes, they can help you, but YOU know YOU better, so make sure you feel confident with yourself when you're following their advice.

My mom believed more in doctors then in herself.

Unfortunately, she fell prey to the "sick care" medical system and their mistake took away her life.

If you follow the doctor's advice and it doesn't help YOU or it makes you worse, YOU are the one left to deal with the repercussions.

PROGRAM YOUR MIND AND EMBRACE YOUR INNER STRENGTH

Your beautiful mind can be like a computer, in that you are downloading information into your mind 24/7.

As the computer that runs your body, it processes whatever information you feed it.

As your mind processes the data, it sends information to your body.

So if you continually look at older people with sadness, despair and shame, then your future as you age will be bleak.

As you age, your mind will be sad and hopelessly thinking about your eventual demise.

You can choose to view others in any way you desire, even if they are old, weak and frail.

Send them love or see them with strength.

What you give out is what you are going to get back.

I was reminded of this recently with my own dad.

After my mother passed away, my dad fell into a deep depression.

We weren't sure if he would make it, as his health was declining.

He was giving up and didn't seem to have a purpose.

I found myself wanting to do more for him so he knew I cared.

I wanted to make beds and help him put things away.

I wanted to DO what I could.

My dad has always been an independent man and this was challenging for both of us.

LOOK FOR EVIDENCE

There were times where I wanted to do so much for him, it irritated him.

In my efforts to help him, I realized I was robbing him of his own power.

He was capable of doing things, and yet I was acting like he was handicapped.

I was treating him the way I saw him.

I decided to change the way I treated and reacted to him.

I saw him with eyes of strength and spoke to him of all I was learning.

I didn't push my beliefs on him.

I simply allowed him to be himself, while sharing my view.

He was intrigued about everything I was learning and became engaged with our conversations.

We went on trips together and although he tired easily, he powered through and kept up as best as he could.

Today my dad is happy and embraces his power (more than he ever did before).

Age has shown itself to him as he abused his body for many years with drugs and alcohol.

He does get tired quicker, yet he doesn't beat himself up as often as he once did.

He looks for evidence to help himself feel better.

It is rewarding for him and those who love him.

LOVING AND ACCEPTING CHANGES TO YOUR BODY AFTER HAVING CHILDREN

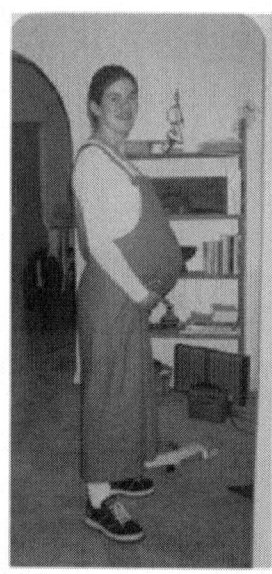 

Ever heard a woman tell you that everything goes downhill after having a baby?

I have.

Some women use this as an excuse to destroy themselves while pregnant, gaining 100 pounds or more.

Being pregnant and eating everything you crave does not mean you will have a healthier baby (or that mama will be healthy).

Some women are conditioned to believe we don't have much control over how our bodies will be after having babies.

Instead of buying into this, I questioned it.

I thought to myself, "Are there women who have not gained lots of weight and stayed healthy overall?"

LOOK FOR EVIDENCE

What if I could have children and still be in amazing physical health?

When I became pregnant at 23, I made a conscious effort to eat healthy and continue to work out.

I went all-in and gained about 30 pounds.

My son weighed 8 pounds and 15 ounces while being 21.5 inches long.

He was big (especially for my size, as I was 5'5" and weighed about 105 pounds before I was pregnant).

With each child, I made sure to pay attention to what I was eating and how I was exercising.

I was active and exercised with each child.

Interestingly enough, I was able to bounce back within a year and get back into shape each time.

After having 3 biological babies, I can tell you I FEEL better than even before I had my babies.

With getting older, I still feel fabulous.

Did my body go through actual changes?

YES!

My body has changed and I honor those changes.

I didn't use any of the changes as an excuse for not honoring my body and taking care of it.

With the birth of my daughter, Alana, I became the proud owner of an umbilical hernia (which happens when you push too hard during labor).

I had surgery soon after to remedy the hernia.

I no longer have a 'perfect' belly button because of the small scar and mesh behind it.

I learned to love the scar and the repaired hernia because it reminds me of delivering my little girl.

The evidence I seek for myself around pregnancy and labor is the gift of my experience.

It is NOT the destruction of my body.

What evidence do you seek for yourself?

Do you look at your body in shame because your skin hangs and you have multiple stretch marks?

If your body has changed because of pregnancy, honor those changes.

Your body is a beautiful temple that housed another human being.

This is SO beautiful.

If you have scars or stretch marks, love what they represent.

Remember: You are the one who decides what they mean to you.

They are your beauty marks.

Loving your body no matter what it looks like will allow your body to heal more productively after pregnancy.

You can even seek out productive evidence around aging too.

Your body and skin change without question.

How will you define these changes, and what will they mean to you?

Will you use aging as a way to break yourself down internally, or will you choose to see yourself with eyes of love?

As you change, look for evidence of women who are active and beautiful.

Women whose age or circumstances doesn't matter to them.

Remember: If you watch a lot of TV, you are being conditioned by society as to what aging means.

I rarely watch TV because I choose not to give permission to anyone else for programming my mind.

Nobody can tell me what it means to age, or what kind of a world we live in.

I am doing what is necessary for me to age effectively and enjoy the process of getting older.

WHAT WILL YOU CHOOSE TO FOCUS ON?

There is an abundance of wisdom we can attain as we age.

This is far more valuable than the attempt to keep our external 'beauty'.

If each woman would invest time every day to go within and KNOW herself, this world would be even more beautiful.

We are emotional creatures.

When left to act on mere emotion, the results can be destructive.

Going within brings such peace because it allows you to be proactive in your physical and mental well-being.

Being proactive about your physical and mental well-being allows you to be more in control of your thoughts.

This doesn't mean you must stand guard on all your thoughts.

It simply means to pay more attention to what evidence you are giving yourself.

Ever heard anyone say "I am having a senior moment" or "Getting older sucks"?

Why would you feed yourself such nonsense?

The more you tell yourself something "getting older sucks" and act like "getting older sucks", the more you will experience it.

If you forget something, perhaps tell yourself, "It's interesting, I usually remember all I need to know."

Why not tell yourself something like "I am getting stronger and stronger every day" or "I am more and more beautiful everyday" instead?

Do you think you are lying to yourself when you say this?

Who said such a thing?

Your mind?

Your husband?

Your doctor?

They don't live in your body.

YOU do.

Speak to yourself and believe the thoughts and words helping you age effectively.

NO ONE CAN ALLOW YOU TO THINK IN A CERTAIN WAY EXCEPT YOU!

There are people who will influence you.

But you are the one who ultimately decides what you will allow to penetrate your mind and soul.

If someone tells you something you don't agree with, then cancel it out by mentally erasing it.

Decide what you allow to replay in your mind.

This takes practice, and although it is easier to react to life, creating your life is much more empowering for yourself.

Ever heard the expression "You get what you focus on"?

If you are focusing on the pain of getting older, then you will experience pain as you get older.

If you focus on the newness and vitality you can experience as you age, then you will be fresh and vibrant.

Change your focus, change your results.

For example...

Someone: Wow, you are old.

You (to yourself): This is their perspective and that's ok...they have a right to their opinion.

I feel amazing.

Then, smile to yourself and mentally delete their comment.

It could be as simple as dismissing it without any acknowledgement.

💡 TIPS FOR CRACKING THE CODE: LOOK FOR EVIDENCE

1 - As you go through your day, notice what is beautiful about yourself and others.

Look at people and see their strengths.

Realize people choose who they are today through their own decisions and actions.

Practicing seeing with eyes of love, rather than judgement and criticism.

This can be hard for women, because at times we feel like we are competing with one another.

Let's say you have been working hard on yourself and your husband takes you out on a date.

You are not quite where you want to be physically, but you're very excited to go out on a date with your husband.

You go to a party and there are several attractive women who look very good in their revealing outfits.

They are obviously single and flirting with almost anyone.

Your head tells you all kinds of things:

They look better than you.

They are going after your husband and are conceited.

They are sluts.

You name it, your head takes you there.

Instead, STOP.

Take a deep breath and talk to yourself.

Tell yourself these ladies are doing the best they can in this moment.

Then take a deep breath, and surround yourself and them with love.

If you are really brave, attempt to talk to them and see if you can get to know them (they may actually be very cool).

Regardless of how they show up, you stay in control of who you are and how you perceive yourself.

This can be challenging if you have wired yourself to be insecure, but each time you practice it and move beyond reacting, you become stronger and stronger.

It can be such a rewarding experience.

2 - Look for a mentor at the age you would feel inspired.

Take them out to lunch from time to time and ask them questions about their life.

See what they have done to be at peace with who they are and what makes them tick.

This is a powerful way to provide evidence to yourself of how someone can age productively.

For what it's worth, my mentor is 85 years old! ;)

3 - Minimize watching TV, your social media time and looking at magazines where other people are attempting to tell you what looks good.

The media attempts to tell us there is value in being young and looking youthful.

Really?

Said who?

Have you ever seen the people who write for the gossip magazines?

They are writing about how horrible someone is dressing, or how much weight they have gained, and yet they are not in shape themselves (mentally or physically).

Remember: You see with your brain, so control what you allow your eyes to see.

Don't give someone else permission to dictate your worth.

4 - Mentor someone.

The best way to learn something is to teach it to others.

Mentor a younger lady who wants your help.

We are all in different seasons of life.

Why not build each other up, rather than tear each other down?

5 - See the strength in situations and people.

Instead of giving out pity or feeling guilty about someone who is in a wheelchair, perhaps think "That is so cool, this person is out and about regardless of any perceived limitations".

Seeing the strength in all people and situations will help you realize there is something strengthening and positive about them.

CHAPTER 5
REDEFINE/RELEASE YOUR PAST

"Holding onto the past is the riskiest choice you can make. Because when you hold onto the past, you erase any chance that you can change."
–Mastin Kipp

What was your childhood like?

When you look back at your childhood, does it make you happy or sad?

Do you have a productive relationship with your parents?

We all have a story about how we were raised and how it has impacted our lives.

Even being raised in the same family can have different stories for each child.

You can have the same parents, yet one child can feel neglected and unloved while the other feels loved and secure.

How we evolve as women depends on what we have told ourselves about our childhood.

Some women are grown adults living as the little girl inside.

These women are scared to be hurt again or fear re-living pains of their past.

Some women may have had an ideal childhood with amazing and nurturing parents.

As a grown adult woman, she may feel her parents' relationship is too hard to achieve, repelling any chance she can of having a productive relationship.

In some ways, a woman with the "perfect dad" can idolize her dad, making it virtually impossible to find the "right" mate.

The stories we tell ourselves are so powerful, and many times we don't even understand we are telling ourselves a story.

If your father left when you were a young child, you might have a story thay says, "Men are selfish and can not be trusted".

This belief can cause you to hate men.

It may also cause you to be in a relationship where you have a selfish husband who cannot be trusted.

If you look at the pattern of your life, you will see the origin of your belief patterns.

It's a hard pill to swallow when we realize our choices have been a direct result of all the stories we continue to tell ourselves.

REDEFINE/RELEASE YOUR PAST

Taking responsibility for how your life has evolved is the first step in creating the life you truly desire.

When tragedy strikes in our lives, we have a tendency to fear this reoccurring.

Ever felt threatened by someone, only to put yourself in "protection mode" over and over again?

The fear associated with this keeps playing like a movie in your head.

This fear builds toxicity (i.e. cortisol, the stress hormone) in your body.

The longer you live in fear, the more toxicity grows and builds up in your body.

Over time, your body will not know how to age effectively because it is accustomed to being in constant breakdown.

If you were raped, molested or abused, do your best to stop having the event replay over and over in your mind.

If you have dismissed the incident as if it never happened yet you still have protective barriers, then you have not truly released the incident.

You are actually feeding it more energy and being victimized by it.

Being a victim robs you of your power.

It depletes you.

Taking responsibility for who you are TODAY and how you define yourself empowers yourself and those around you.

Taking responsibility does not mean you are blaming yourself for the horrific incident.

It means you won't allow it to continue to victimize you.

Forgive the incident and attacker.

Forgiving the person who attacked you does not mean you condone their behavior, nor are you asking for it to happen again to you.

It means you are releasing the chains that energetically bind you to this person/event/situation.

I understand this sounds easier said than done.

It will take work.

You are worthy enough to let go of any situation that does not allow you to live life to your fullest potential.

Do what is necessary to move beyond the incident.

The more you replay the incident, the more power you feed the situation.

However horrific the situation was, it happened in the past.

Release it.

Do your best to move beyond it and redefine who you are.

Tell yourself you are stronger because the incident happened to you.

The more you convince yourself of your strength, the more you will release the power the incident has on your being.

We have fabulous resources available to us today.

Find a good therapist.

Join a self-help group.

Invest in a self-help course.

You won't ever be able to control the past yet you can control what it means to you.

Acting like a negative incident never happened and not allowing yourself to heal is only masking the problem.

This will only cause issues later down the road as you age.

Clearing your emotional and physical body of the pain will bring you freedom and peace.

The way you age will be positively affected.

You will even feel like a huge burden/weight has been lifted from your being.

EMBRACING THE DEATH OF LOVED ONES

Losing a loved one can make it hard to want to go on.

Death can leave us feeling paralyzed.

As we get older, people we love die before we do.

This often makes us feel empty and alone.

This can be extremely challenging, as we love whomever passed on.

There is often a huge void in our life.

It is painful and the pain can linger.

It's important for your health and well-being to do what you can to move beyond their passing.

Look at how you can grow because of their physical loss.

I am not suggesting you discount what they meant to you.

I am suggesting you change the meaning of not physically having them with you any longer.

With the tragic loss of my mom, I have trained myself to shift my perspective when my mind attempts to shower me with guilt or sadness.

I speak to my mom.

I know she is with me and I act as such.

I ask for signs and she reveals them to me.

Think I'm crazy?

You can and have every right to think I am crazy.

I am happily living my life in the most productive way I know how.

What could you do to live the remaining years of your life as productively as possible without your loved one physically with you?

If they truly loved you, they want you to live the rest of this physical life with joy.

They want you to move beyond the pain and grow your emotional muscles by productively living your life.

If your deceased loved one could speak to you in this very moment, do you think they would say, "I love you and I want you to live the remainder of your years filled with joy"?

Or do you think they would say, "I want you to suffer every day because I am not with you".

Don't live the rest of your life unhappy.

REDEFINING MISTAKES YOU HAVE MADE IN THE PAST

If you're like me, you have screwed up plenty of times in your life.

Some of those memories will creep into my head, and depending on how long I focus on it, I can become sad and/or depressed.

My head attempts to have feelings of guilt and condemnation run through my body.

Those feelings often make a person feel stuck and inadequate.

Not one of us will do this life journey absolutely "perfect".

Feeling guilty won't help you age effectively.

Therefore, know when you can improve and take action toward improving every day.

We put ourselves on vicious cycles of self-defeating mental attacks, thinking we have to torture ourselves for our behavior.

STOP!

The best thing you can do for yourself and the aging process is to learn and decide to become better and stronger.

Don't allow others to 'make' you feel guilty.

If you have family members who have a patterned behavior of poking the guilt stick at you, then do your best to distance yourself from them (or don't allow the guilt stick to penetrate you).

Choose who and what you allow into this life journey with you.

When redefining your past, pay attention to how you are defining the future for those you care about.

I have witnessed women who have illnesses they project onto their children:

- "I hope you don't get this".
- "When I was your age, I was healthy too."
- Your grandma and aunt died of breast cancer, be careful because you will get it too."

We have no idea how powerful our words can be, especially when used around impressionable children.

Be cautious about the words you choose when dealing with your children or family.

Your children will listen to the words you say and how you say them.

REDEFINE/RELEASE YOUR PAST

If you are continually looking to your children for strength to move past your sickness, then it is likely they can develop the sickness too.

Remember what I told you earlier about researchers studying cancer who eventually end up getting the same cancer?

The more someone immerses themselves without a way to release, the more likely they will become what they are immersed in.

Allow the past to stay in the past.

Don't allow yourself to live a 'life sentence' by the prison bars of the past.

Be present to the magnificence of life in this moment.

Tomorrow is not promised for any of us, therefore being a negative future prophesier won't help you crack the "Fountain of Youth" code.

Let me tell you about my own experience with being locked in the past and how I eventually overcame it.

Growing up without a father, I was one of your typical girls who had "daddy" issues.

I had no idea what it was like to have a productive relationship with a man.

For me, men could not be trusted but were needed.

I felt like I needed to have a man, but was not worthy enough to keep a man (after all, my dad left me and my siblings at an early age).

As a young teenage girl, I prayed to God to find a man who would love me with all my flaws.

The first young man who paid attention to me won my heart, or at least because my mind told me I needed him.

"Wow, someone actually likes me with all these flaws?"

I felt like this was as good as it is going to get.

Did it matter that he didn't graduate from high school? No.

Did it matter that he smoked marijuana before every movie to make sure he could enjoy it? No.

Did it matter that he didn't have a steady job? No.

What mattered is he "loved" me.

In my head, I thought I had to do all I could to make sure I kept him.

At 18, he was my first boyfriend and I was with him for almost 5 years, marrying him when I was 22 years old.

We bought our first home before we were married.

When he did work, I would wake up at 4:30 am in the morning, make him his breakfast and lunch, and started his car in the morning so it would be warm for him when he left.

I wanted to be the "perfect" wife for him.

Sadly, he took much for granted and was not motivated.

When things got tough, he wouldn't look for extra work, so I had 3 jobs at one point in the relationship just so we could pay the bills.

I created a living environment that was not sustainable for me.

I felt like a slave to someone who was using me.

Ultimately, after 21 years of being together and 17 years of marriage with 3 beautiful children, I had enough.

I didn't want to be used any longer.

Was this all his fault?

No.

Did I make lots of mistakes in this marriage?

Too many to list.

At the end of the marriage, I gave him the house, belongings, vehicles, our savings accounts, and I felt as if I lost my family.

I took the debt and my clothes with a mutual agreement; the children would have split time between us.

After 2.5 years of being separated and no real written agreement from him on the divorce, I finally began to date.

When I met my current husband, Jay, my ex-husband made sure to do all he could to tarnish my name.

I even lost my middle son for 5 years as he wanted nothing to do with me during this time. My whole family, with the exception of my younger brother, turned against me. My sister, who I was close to growing up, became my enemy. My own mother alienated me (and died during this time).

I was required to pay child and spousal support because I was the one who hustled (earning much more income than he did).

Those days were the darkest times in my life.

I looked for ways to take my life.

I didn't want to give him any more gratification of using and "torturing" me.

Thankfully I didn't follow through with what my ego mind was telling me.

It did get better.

Was it because my ex-husband was a nicer person? No.

He still blames me for the breakdown of our relationship and won't communicate with me.

In his mind, I set him up for an easy life then took it all away from him.

I don't wish him any ill will.

I send him love energetically and pray for him to have peace.

I do this because it makes me feel better.

Regardless of the breakdown of our relationship, he is the father of my children and I ultimately want him to live a good life.

I don't live in the past any longer.

How our divorce evolved is a good story to tell, yet it doesn't define me.

I have invested a lot of time to truly appreciate who I am.

I have come to honor my journey.

If my ex-husband chooses to be resentful and angry, he has every right to be miserable.

It is not my job to make him happy or understand how he thinks.

It is my job to create a story that will allow me to be productive for myself, my husband, and my children.

After all, when mama is happy, everyone is happy :)

REDEFINE/RELEASE YOUR PAST

💡 TIPS FOR CRACKING THE CODE: REDEFINE YOUR PAST

1 – Go back to when you were a little girl.

What was your earliest recollection of a time where you felt lost, lonely, or incomplete?

How did you define this?

How are you being this in your life now?

What changes can you make to empower yourself beyond this belief?

As an example, my earliest recollection was when I was a little girl – maybe 3 years old, looking out our large front window.

My dad was leaving (probably the one time my mom let him stay over) and I was crying as I watched him go into his car.

I recall feeling like I was not worthy enough to have my own dad stay in my life.

I felt like I was a piece of trash.

For many years after that event, I created my fundamental misperception.

I believed the statement: "I am a piece of trash".

I worked hard to prove I wasn't a piece of trash by excelling in school or being the "good" child.

I chose a man I had to work hard to keep, just to prove I wasn't a piece of trash.

I would allow other people to disrespect me, because after all, I was a piece of trash!

It wasn't until my late 30s where my awareness to this belief came at a Matthew Ferry seminar.

The moment I realized this, tears streamed down my face and I felt the biggest release of negativity from my soul.

In that very moment, I finally felt worthy.

It was one of the most beautiful moments I have ever experienced.

Today, I can have an awareness of how I am showing up in my life.

I am now in a relationship where my husband truly honors me.

I allow our children to do more for themselves, rather than have them depend on me so I can feel significant.

Honoring and valuing who I am feels so much better than living in fear or unworthiness.

2 – STOP bringing up the pain of the past to people you care about.

Leave the past where it belongs: In the past.

Continually bringing up past pains to instill guilt into others not only takes away your power, but causes other people to not want to be around you.

When you tell someone you forgive them, FORGIVE them.

Forgiveness does not mean you keep the past pain in your memory bank.

It also doesn't mean constantly reminding the person about how you were hurt.

3 – If you have been abused (molested, raped, etc.), write a letter to your attacker.

Put all of your feelings and memories about the event in a letter.

Make it as long or as short as needed to allow you to feel like you are releasing it.

Cry and be angry.

Once you are done writing the letter, read it as if you are an outside observer.

Don't view it as if you are a participant within it.

Visually step outside and bring zero emotion into it.

As the observer, bless yourself and your attacker.

Then, burn the letter.

Release the event.

Do your best to act like it was just a movie you watched.

NOTE: Being raped, molested and/or abused is a tragic event. Allowing it to replay over and over again in your mind only gives the occurrence more power. It is like you were abused multiple, multiple times.

Do NOT allow this event to dictate how the rest of your life plays out.

You can decide to tell yourself a different story about this event.

It takes strength, courage and practice.

I promise you that telling yourself the same victimized story over and over again will never serve you.

4 – If you have lost your partner (i.e. the love of your life) and you are feeling lonely, remind yourself that they haven't left you.

If you haven't seen the movie GHOST, I highly recommend watching it.

Think of your loved one as the husband who passed away.

Talk to them.

Ask them to give you a sign.

When my mom was alive, she often told me that if a hummingbird flew close to you, it was the sign of a deceased loved one being near.

When I ask my mom for a sign, I have had numerous occasions where a hummingbird flew right next to me as if to tell me my mom is nearby.

My mom is with me.

I can feel her love.

CHAPTER 6
FORGIVE AND RELEASE RESENTMENTS

"Forgive others not because they deserve forgiveness but because you Deserve peace"
−Jonathan Lockwood Huie

This chapter is similar to the previous one.

I wanted the subject of forgiveness to have its own chapter.

This is where most women have the greatest challenge: Actually forgiving and releasing resentments.

If you are breathing, you have been hurt (physically or emotionally) in your life.

The quality of your life will depend on the length of time you've let this pain penetrate you.

Pain is an inevitable part of life. Avoiding pain or acting like it won't affect you disempowers you.

Unfortunately, some hold onto this resentment for years or their entire lifetime.

This only ages us faster.

We turn this pain into a 'story', thereby validating the reasons we remain the way we are.

This 'story' becomes more important than the quality of our life.

Since the experience was in the past, it no longer exists today.

We give it power when we replay it in our mind and/or explain it to others.

Retelling the story from the point of pain positions us as a pure victim.

This victim position then becomes part of our identity.

We believe this is who we are and it becomes harder to change.

In life, there are two types of identity consciousness.

'Victim Consciousness' is when one blames everything and everybody else for their issues.

When they finally pull themselves up by the bootstraps, they latch onto their 'savior' or 'guru' because that person (in their mind) will be responsible for saving them.

'Empowered Consciousness' is a person who realizes they are responsible for every action they have ever taken and get to choose how they want to live their life.

I would hope you see the correct identity consciousness template to emulate.

RESOLVING CHILDHOOD TRAUMA AND ABANDONMENT

"I am this way because I never had a father".

Really?

You cannot change NOW because you didn't have a father over 30 years ago?

If you believe this, then it is true for you because you are stuck in victim/savior consciousness.

Many women have "daddy issues" because their father wasn't around.

They continue to relive their fear of abandonment by participating in unproductive relationships or simply 'hating' the men they choose.

Unresolved "daddy" issues cause women to struggle with relationships and self-worth.

The only true way to resolve their issues is through forgiveness.

Many of the "daddy" issues are due to what we are told by whomever raised us (usually our mother) while our father was not present.

If we were raised with the story of "Your dad is such a loser and he abandoned us", then you will have ingrained abandonment beliefs.

If your father wasn't around when you were growing up, ask yourself what were you told.

How is your relationship with people of the opposite sex?

Let's be clear: Not having a father affected you as a child.

But accepting this truth can be a powerful tool for creating emotional growth in your life.

The experience can allow you to have more compassion for others.

There are true gifts in all the experiences of life.

You must choose to see the gift in the situation.

Give yourself the gift of reflection.

Reflect on how you are defining your childhood and how it is affecting you as a grown woman.

It's OK to understand you struggled and admit it.

It's OK to not hold onto the pain of your childhood.

It's OK to realize you are a different person now than when you were a child.

Reflecting and releasing can lift years of burden off of your body.

This will allow you to age more effectively.

Emotional pain from your childhood is real.

It feels deep because we anchored these feelings when they occurred.

FORGIVE AND RELEASE RESENTMENTS

Think about it: As a child, you are easily influenced and moldable.

You are this little being who is innocent and filled with love, life and curiosity.

Then someone you trusted and loved let you down.

They leave or abuse you.

You are left feeling despondent and alone.

Due to this pain and trauma, you now protect yourself vigilantly.

You now struggle to allow yourself to give and receive love.

Feeling unloved, you unconsciously choose ways to destroy yourself and your relationships.

Many women suffering in this fashion drink, use drugs, or spend money excessively in an attempt to mask their real issue, lack of love and self-worth.

Forgiving someone does not mean you are saying what they did was OK.

Forgiveness is releasing a cord of attachment and/ or any energy you have attached to them.

Most women don't realize the simple act of forgiveness frees them of bondage.

Many women are not taught how to forgive.

We are instead taught how to be angry and how to resent those who harmed us.

And more often than not, how to ignore the issue or the primary person involved.

Here are some questions to reflect on if you felt abandoned in your childhood:

- *What was I told about my father (or even mother) not being around?*
- *Was I adopted? What is the story I tell myself around my adoption?*
- *If my father wasn't around, how did my mother speak about him?*
- *What was the story I was told about why they left? (Most times, our mothers tell the story from their perspective, which is from their own pain)*
- *Am I holding onto a story told from someone else's perspective?*
- *Do I still want to live as this scared, unloved little girl?*
- *Where can I let go of any unproductive beliefs I developed as a little girl around feeling unworthy or unloved?*
- *I was abused (physically, mentally, sexually). What story do you tell yourself about this abuse? Are you defined by it? Do you tell yourself you are a survivor continuously, thereby identifying yourself because of this abuse?*

Questioning your beliefs will allow you to investigate why you think and act the way you do.

You are NOT a problem to be solved!

I like to think of each woman as a beautiful treasure to be found.

It can take some work to dig for the treasure.

When one finally digs deep enough, what is found is more beautiful than anyone can imagine.

As parents, we don't realize the best thing we can do for our children is to teach them how to forgive.

Allow your children to see you feel hurt, and then let them see you forgive (i.e. forgive yourself and others).

Teach them how forgiveness does not mean you allow this situation back into your life.

You don't have to give someone permission to come back into your life and use you.

Forgiveness can show itself in many ways and depends on each circumstance.

It means not allowing someone or something to emotionally affect you.

Having supreme control over your emotional state allows you to crack the "Fountain of Youth" code at will.

USING FORGIVENESS TO BECOME A VICTOR INSTEAD OF A VICTIM

Think of your body as a storehouse of all your emotions.

The more you allow yourself to feel, forgive, and release your emotions, the more you allow the energy to move through your body.

When you hold onto pain from the past, you block the flow, thereby causing the "clog" in your body.

This "clog" can develop into a tumor or other illnesses, depending on the depth of the pain and how long it's been held onto.

Being a victim disempowers anyone.

The moment you take full responsibility for your life by forgiving yourself and others is the moment you regain your power.

No one is responsible for you.

Only you can decide who you will be and how you will show up regardless of your life's circumstances.

Taking full responsibility does not mean you have to blame yourself for all your problems.

Blaming and responsibility are two very different things.

Blame puts up the defenses and is demeaning, whereas responsibility empowers and uplifts.

If you have been a victim for most of your life, this pain has become your friend.

It will feel comfortable to feel the pain while being angry with others.

You won't know how to live without the pain as it has become your normal way of life.

This is a common reason as to why some people stay in abusive relationships.

The pain is what is familiar and comfortable.

Living in the pain can also give people great meaning in their life.

They become attached to the drama and/or pain because it gives them the attention they desire.

"Poor Jennifer, she is stuck in that marriage because of those kids."

FORGIVE AND RELEASE RESENTMENTS

"I can't believe Samantha's dad never calls her for her birthday, she must be heartbroken."

Feeding into the drama gives the negative situation more energy.

Tragically, some like receiving this kind of attention more than being happy and free.

When pain is not dealt with and left stuck in emotional body centers, it will age you faster and make one mentally and/or physically sick.

If forgiveness could be stuffed into a pill, it would be the magic elixir to help women and men age more effectively.

However, life is not that easy.

Putting in the effort to forgive strengthens your emotional and physical body.

The simple act of forgiveness can heal you, far beyond your comprehension.

If you have never been taught how to forgive, forgiveness takes real work.

Forgiveness can be made in a moment, or you may have to dig deep within and revisit pivotal events in your life.

Feel those events, forgive them, and let them go.

Experiment with what works for you.

You live in your body, and only you know what is working or what is not.

You can work through the issues on your own, or you may need the help of a professional therapist.

If you go to a therapist, make sure you interview them to feel comfortable and safe.

Regardless of how you approach learning forgiveness, the choice is yours to do the work necessary to move beyond your resentments, and actually forgive and release any/all negative experiences weighing you down.

I went to several self-help classes and spiritual seminars to help release my emotional baggage.

I can tell you without hesitation that the moment I released my emotional baggage, I felt free.

I felt 10 years younger.

I felt like I could accomplish anything.

I felt powerful and beautiful for the first time in my life.

This is THE GOLDEN KEY to cracking the "Fountain of Youth" code.

To age effectively, YOU MUST release your emotional baggage.

Many of us are making decisions based on ONE incident (or several) and allowing it to dictate who we are.

If this is you, you've likely built up protection mechanisms to ensure the hurt will NEVER be felt again.

Yet the pain is still there.

It is a vicious and potentially never-ending cycle of abusive relationships, drug abuse, and alcoholism.

In other words, a life of pure hell.

Not releasing this pain allows it to have power over you.

It will negatively affect you and noticeably age your body.

We become scared of having to resolve the pain and fear.

But what if we could instead allow ourselves to simply become comfortable with the pain, thereby allowing us to move beyond it?

Women who refuse to release their emotional baggage continually seek approval from others and society.

They are embracing the victim identity consciousness, looking for someone/something to make them "whole".

These women often have one plastic surgery operation after the other, looking for a way to feel better.

They continue to look in the mirror and see themselves with eyes of sadness/disgust.

Seeing yourself with fear, pity and/or condemnation will NEVER allow you to see your true beauty.

When you see your true beauty, you remove years of aging off your face.

It is NOT due to your latest wrinkle-erasing injection session, but your fresh and accepting eyes.

Learn how to redefine situations in your life to help you release the pain.

Resistance rewards pain, whereas forgiveness heals it.

HOW I FINALLY LET GO OF MY OWN EMOTIONAL BAGGAGE AND STARTED LOVING MY DAD AGAIN

My mom and dad had 4 children within 3 years,

My dad was an alcoholic, lost and afraid in those days, which caused him to leave us when my youngest brother (the fourth child) was only 3 weeks old.

Thankfully, he has been sober for 36 years now (It makes me very proud he was able to overcome his addiction).

We would see him on occasion when he'd come back, attempting to act like we were a family.

He would then get drunk and disappear.

I grew up hating my dad.

I hated him being around.

I hated who he represented.

I hated him not being present in my life.

FORGIVE AND RELEASE RESENTMENTS

I hated not having a "normal" family.

My father eventually got sober when I was in middle school.

When someone gets sober and they attempt to live life without alcohol, they can be irritable (at least my dad was).

My mom allowed him back since he decided to get sober, and they attempted to restart life together.

Because my mom was on welfare when we were young, my dad had to pay all the money back to the government.

He worked out of our house as an appraiser and worked his butt off.

He was determined to make amends and pay off all his debts.

Because he was so focused on paying off his debts, he seemingly hated us making noises or bothering him.

We constantly had to walk on eggshells while he was working.

My dad would have outbursts around my friends for various reasons, even for insignificant things like someone parking in his parking spot on the driveway.

I was embarrassed by my dad and never completely understood him.

I blamed him for many of my issues and for the terrible way (in my eyes) he treated my mom.

Upon graduating from high school and with no real direction in my life, I decided to work with my him by becoming a Certified Residential Appraiser.

Working for my dad was not fun.

I must have been fired 3 times but I kept going back because I had no self-worth.

Plus, I needed a job.

Fortunately, the longer I worked with my dad, the more I began to understand him.

I realized he just wanted love and had no idea how to express his need for love.

His way of expressing his need was to have outbursts and act like a jerk.

He simply didn't know another way.

When I had my own children, I realized how difficult it is to be a parent.

In my early 30s, I was fortunate to enroll in a self-mastery course which allowed me to take responsibility for my side of a relationship.

I realized my dad was doing the best he knew how with the tools he had.

I also realized that being a parent is one of the toughest jobs there is.

As most of you know, there is no written instructional manual for being a parent.

My Dad was not given a guide to raising me.

He wasn't a reader, and would never have read one anyway.

When I finally took responsibility for my relationship with my Dad, I knew I had to forgive him and myself.

I now view our relationship with true freedom from suffering.

My experience with my father was a story I told myself.

The story I told myself for years was that my dad was a jerk and didn't care about anyone but himself.

I blamed him for my lack of self-worth.

If I would have had a father involved in my life, then I could have valued who I was.

But playing the blame game never helps and often makes the issue worse.

By forgiving my dad for the breakdown in our relationship, I realized I had the power to improve it.

I showed up in a more loving way to my dad and my dad showed up loving to me in return.

Granted, he didn't always show up as I expected.

But he was an improved version of who he was previously.

Accepting him unconditionally helped him to see that my forgiveness was genuine.

I'm very proud to say we now have a great relationship.

I feel truly blessed to have my dad as my father.

Most people are reacting to life.

Most people don't stop and ask themselves how they are showing up to other people.

Something happens and they get happy or sad.

We live our lives getting upset with other people because they aren't showing up how we want them to.

We won't forgive them because (in our own minds) they hurt us too much.

Holding onto that pain is only hurting YOU.

THIS EMOTIONAL PAIN AGES YOU FAST!

THIS EMOTIONAL PAIN BREAKS YOUR BODY DOWN.

Crack the "Fountain of Youth" code by forgiving yourself and others.

 TIPS FOR CRACKING THE CODE: FORGIVE AND RELEASE RESENTMENTS

1 - Take full responsibility for your life.

Stop playing victim to anything or anyone in your life.

Are you in a crappy relationship?

Look at the relationship and your part in it.

If you are being abused, then take responsibility for staying in the relationship.

If you are in a relationship with a weak person who you have no respect for, take responsibility for how you treat them.

This DOES NOT mean you will allow people to disrespect you.

This only means you take responsibility for how your life is evolving.

Only you can create real change in your life.

If you are in an unproductive relationship with no hope for improving, take full responsibility and leave.

2 - Take action toward improving your life.

Once you have taken responsibility, do something to focus on healing.

Mentally forgive yourself for how your relationship has turned out.

Have you been impatient with people at work?

FORGIVE AND RELEASE RESENTMENTS

Take responsibility for showing up as a jerk and change your attitude toward people.

If you are in an abusive relationship, leave.

This will feel uncomfortable because it won't feel normal.

Keep at it and see how others show up.

The world is a reflection of us.

When we are kind, the world seems kinder.

When we are fearful, the world seems scary.

When we are at peace, the world is beautiful.

Think of the world as a true cosmic mirror.

We always reflect back what we give off.

Remembering this is the first step to real and effective change in our life.

3 - If someone cuts you off in traffic today, don't cuss them out.

Do your best to simply forgive them and move on.

Do not allow them to upset you.

Be in control of who you are and how you react.

4 - Call, text, or write a letter to someone who you haven't forgiven and/or you still have resentment toward.

NOTE: If this is someone who raped, molested, or attempted to physically hurt you, then you don't have to have any physical communication with them.

If you can speak to them, apologize for your part in the relationship.

It could be you reliving this incident and continually being a victim to the situation.

Ask them how they viewed the relationship.

They may not show up as you want, and that is okay.

Don't set yourself up expecting them to break down and tell you they want forgiveness from you.

This is for YOU, not for them.

If speaking to them causes more harm than good, don't speak to them.

You know your situation best.

If you are not physically communicating with this person, you may feel it's best to write a letter instead.

Once you are done writing the letter, read it out loud (as if you are reading it to them) and release them from the chains you have created.

Then tear up the letter, and either burn it in a safe place or throw it away.

You can even close your eyes and picture the person in your mind's eye.

Picture speaking to them and energetically forgiving them.

Surround them and yourself in love.

Allow yourself to feel the peace of forgiveness.

5 - STOP playing the blame game.

Many times, we attempt to blame someone for 'wronging' us.

"How could they have done this?"

We go to other people, seeking validation about how we feel so we have more evidence about how crappy this other person is.

If this is your habit, then stop yourself immediately.

Playing the 'blame game' won't help you crack the "Fountain of Youth" code.

It will only cause more resistance in your body, and the remainder of your years will be a struggle.

If you enjoy struggling, then keep blaming.

If you don't, then stop blaming other people.

Take ownership for your life and how it is evolving.

6 - If you are a parent, teach your child about forgiveness by allowing them to see you forgive.

Have a discussion with them about what it means to forgive someone.

Let them see you in action, picking up the phone or talking to somebody in person.

Our children do not learn from what we say as much as what we DO.

They are amazing little observers and mimics.

If you tell your children about the importance of forgiveness, make sure they see you carrying out forgiveness to yourself and others.

This will definitely help you as you age.

Getting older with your children, knowing they know how to forgive, will help you be much happier and at peace.

It isn't fun getting older when our children continue to blame or hold resentment against us.

CHAPTER 7
THERE IS NO COMPARISON

"Comparison is the thief of joy"
-Theodore Roosevelt

There is only ONE YOU.

No other person looks exactly like you, or is made up with your exact DNA.

Why do you think DNA testing is so accurate?

Your blueprint can be similar to someone else's, but it will never be an exact duplicate.

Yes, there is only ONE YOU!

So why do we compare ourselves to others?

Aging doesn't help the cause.

We may walk out of the house feeling pretty good for a night out on the town.

We go out, and there is this hotty-totty little young thing strutting her stuff, turning the heads of all the men around her (including your man, or the person you are with).

Looking at her, your self-worth crumbles about 10 notches.

Why does your self-worth need to crumble when this hotty-totty thing comes around?

> **Your self-worth only crumbles because you are comparing yourself to her, then sprinkling it with judgement shots.**

Interestingly enough, we create stories in our minds about who people are.

Ironically, most people are much more concerned about themselves than they will be about you.

We act like every person around us is looking at and judging us.

Even if they are, their opinion is none of your business.

Everyone will have an opinion.

You never have to agree with anyone's opinion.

COMPARING YOURSELF TO OTHERS IS THE GAME YOU NEVER WIN, NO MATTER HOW LONG YOU PLAY

Measuring yourself against someone else is an exercise in futility.

EVEN if you think you look better, you're just trying to make one right and the other wrong.

Who said you both can't be beautiful?

Life is not a beauty pageant; it's a pageant to express your beauty.

External beauty fades, no matter how many plastic surgeries you have.

True beauty is expressed by who you are and not what you look like.

One woman's beauty does not automatically invalidate your own beauty.

You have been conditioned to think otherwise.

If you have been conditioned to think 'younger is better', then why not recondition yourself to think 'older is better'?

The comparison game can begin as early as in our childhood, and the conditioning is hard to break.

Ever had your parent(s) say, "Why can't you be more like so-and-so?"

Ever had your friends say, "Mary is so cool and she has a big house"?

Ever heard your teacher say "Look at John, he is so smart and knows all the answers. Why don't you?"

From a young age, we are taught to compare ourselves to others.

In some ways, this can cause us to want to be better.

However, in many ways this causes us to feel like we are not enough.

The comparison game we play causes us to compete with others, which separates and divides people.

If we could all cooperate with one another, there would be a stronger sense of unity among us as a species.

With respect to aging, comparing adds zero value to helping you age effectively.

Compare facts and figures all you want.

If you're going to compare how you look or feel with someone else, make sure to do it in a way that uplifts you.

Demeaning other people will never uplift you.

When your mind is in comparison mode, it can take you all over the place.

Stand in line at the grocery store and look at the magazines.

Compare yourself to the 'perfect' look of celebrities, and you start to feel inadequate.

THERE IS NO COMPARISON

We watch TV shows about celebrities who live fabulous lives because our own lives aren't so hot.

We scroll through social media, looking at how 'perfect' everyone else's lives are while ours is mediocre at best.

All of this is merely a facade.

But in our minds, we think it is real.

We then beat ourselves up because our own lives are not so perfect.

Our mind can be our own worst enemy when left to its own devices.

Thoughts of unworthiness and doubt easily creep in.

Without continual inner awareness, we can be mentally torn down by our own mind.

It's important to train yourself to question thoughts that don't help you feel strong or worthy.

We all have something we don't like about ourselves.

When someone points out one of our insecurities, it will often magnify the issue.

However, learning how to love your perceived flaws will remedy the issue.

Instead of comparing, appreciate someone else's life as being good.

Be happy for anyone who is happy.

It's OK to celebrate seeing other people live a great life.

Your mind will give you feedback about people and situations.

That is the job of the mind.

Learn to stop and pay attention to what your mind is telling you.

It is protecting you by pointing out what is wrong with yourself, people and situations.

The mind is doing its job.

Fighting or resisting it does you no good.

Your mind has a purpose, otherwise we would not have one.

Learn how to use your mind in a productive way.

If it wants to tear others down, investigate why your mind is attempting to protect you.

Ask your mind this empowering question: What is going on?

Are you feeling insecure?

Are you not loving fully?

HOW TO ACCEPT YOURSELF WITHOUT NEEDING EXTERNAL APPROVAL FROM SOCIETY

If your mind is more concerned about what others think, then realize your mind is attempting to protect you.

THERE IS NO COMPARISON

Is this a signal to be more comfortable in your own skin?

Are you seeking external approval rather than accepting yourself?

Think about it this way: Why do you think todays 'selfie' game is so strong?

People are attempting to feel significant and beautiful in the eyes of others.

Many post 'selfies' in anticipation of how many likes and comments they will get.

This is a very dangerous game if you define your self-worth by it.

It leaves many women constantly logging into their social media accounts, becoming less and less productive.

Social media has created a "make believe" world for many of us to live in.

Since we have become a society based on external approval, many of us use an infinite number of digital editing tools to change any part of ourselves that is "wrong".

For instance, many women become obsessed with having plastic surgery to fix all their perceived imperfections.

There is a surgery for almost anything today.

Many women will 'feel' better about themselves on the surface while never addressing the underlying core issue of insecurity.

Plastic surgery is a wonderful gift for many people.

My personal opinion is that people who get plastic surgery with the hope of fixing all their issues will realize it can be a never-ending search for 'perfection'.

This perfection is unattainable because they don't love or accept themselves.

If plastic surgery was mixed with therapy or a self-improvement class, I could see the procedures succeeding more.

If we don't love and approve of ourselves internally, then how can having external plastic surgery remedy this?

If we don't love and approve of ourselves, then how can taking pictures with filters remedy this?

How can make-up remedy this?

All of these things offer temporary solutions to real issues.

They can and do offer quick remedies.

If we don't strengthen our self-love muscles, then no matter how "beautiful" you think you are, it is only temporary.

Love yourself simply because you are who you are.

If you decide to have plastic surgery, wear makeup or post filtered pics, these things can enhance your being.

However, regularly using filters often makes us become virtually unrecognizable in person.

Ever run into someone in person who you only knew from social media and could not even recognize who they were?

This is the time we live in.

We are not honest with ourselves, making it a challenge to be honest with others.

You don't have to be called a "catfish" because you are unrecognizable.

It's like we all know we are being lied to, but it's OK because everyone does it.

Look at what sells to help people look better or younger.

There are pills, creams, shots, treatments.

It's a billion-dollar business preying on our insecurities.

We are shown "touched up" pictures of women who use a certain cream or treatment.

And then there's the comparison of how we look compared to the perfect image.

It is hard to live up to the expectations given to us by marketing companies.

Think about it: Marketing companies have people who strategize on how to sell the most amount of product they possibly can to insecure people.

These insecure people are the ones who will pay LOTS of money to look better because deep down inside they don't like who they are.

A better remedy would be to invest time and energy into accepting and honoring who YOU are, loving yourself for all your perceived imperfections.

Sure, go ahead and work to improve your appearance.

It's human nature to want to be better and improve, but it doesn't mean you believe you are NOT enough.

If you were to get one message from this book, it should be this: Know how fabulous it is to be YOU!

The truth is that we are all beautiful when viewed from the whole perspective.

Sadly, many of us won't express or show our true beauty to the world.

I am not referring to what we look like without make-up.

I am referring to our true essence which lies beneath the surface.

True beauty penetrates and stays with people long after the person leaves our presence.

A woman who understands her beauty is a bright light who strengthens all those around her.

Even the thought of this woman can strengthen people.

External beauty cannot do this.

Sure, it can stimulate someone, but external beauty is only on-the-surface and won't last forever.

WHAT IF MY HUSBAND LEAVES ME FOR A YOUNGER WOMAN?

Ever heard of a couple married for years, and then the man leaves her for a younger woman?

I have heard of this happening many times.

Although each situation can be different, I would infer that older men typically leave a relationship when the "fun" and acceptance has dissipated from the relationship.

There is no unconditional love for each other.

Usually, one or both partners have conditional love (i.e. "do this for me or I won't respect you").

The wife may stop having sex with her husband and start complaining about who he is.

THERE IS NO COMPARISON

The man grows weary of the treatment by his wife.

Out of nowhere, a younger woman comes along with a freshness and sensuality he has not felt for years.

It then becomes easy for the man to be a part of this younger woman's life.

He craves this feeling as it becomes addictive, since it has been lost from his current relationship.

Do you want your relationship to last?

Keep the freshness alive in your relationship.

Accept your partner for who they are.

Tell your husband and/or others what you love about him.

Invest time for him and your relationship.

Be the magnetic woman you once were.

Bring some mystery and freedom into your relationship.

He doesn't have to be anyone but himself for you to love him.

Seek your inner wisdom and share this with your love.

He will find it invaluable.

Is this a 100% guarantee that an older man won't leave his wife for a younger woman?

There are no guarantees in life.

This is why it's important for you to love and honor yourself while being the best possible partner you can be.

You can only control your side of the street.

If a man decides he wants to leave for a younger woman, then bless him and be grateful he left.

He was only meant to be on your journey for a certain amount of time.

He has his own lessons in life.

If a man only values a woman because of her age, is this a man you want to be with?

Not one of us is more valuable than the other, young or old.

If there is a perceived value because of age or level of success, it is just a story we've told ourselves.

We are all human beings.

Our worth is not based on our age or our level of success.

Wouldn't it be cool to start viewing our worth by how much value we bring to the world?

Our value would be based on how much we love ourselves and others unconditionally.

This would alleviate the pressure we feel as we age when we compare ourselves to younger women.

And guess what?

Younger women, if fortunate, will get older one day too.

They will learn how to love and accept themselves unconditionally.

If you want to stop the comparison game, then your best strategy is to work on your inner game.

Strengthen your self-love muscles and KNOW your own worth.

Get back to knowing your partner again (if you are in a relationship).

THERE IS NO COMPARISON

Cooperate with others.

Stop competing.

Being a woman is fabulous, especially when we allow our divine goddess to shine through.

Accept your beauty and power.

There is beauty and mystery that can engage any partner when a goddess woman fully expresses her power.

Is it easy?

No.

It takes practice.

You have spent years practicing to be how you are today.

It will take time to change any old habits.

Be patient and kind to yourself as you maneuver through the process of finding your sparkle and shine.

Let go of comparing.

Be free and have fun!

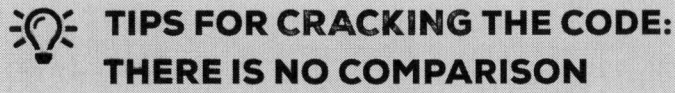

TIPS FOR CRACKING THE CODE: THERE IS NO COMPARISON

1 – Practice accepting others and yourself for who you are.

Look at others and yourself with eyes of love.

Know that we are all doing the best we can at any given moment.

Like my mentor Matthew Ferry always tells me, "Practice total and complete acceptance of all people, in all situations, at all times, including yourself."

2 – Journal each day or night (or whenever you can) about the things you like about yourself, or are improving.

You can keep track of how you are doing when you finish your journal.

It can be a fun way to see how far you have come.

I use a composition notebook for my daily journaling.

I sometimes glance at my entries before I throw them away. Sometimes I just throw them away without looking to show myself I know I am better than I was yesterday.

3 – Stop telling yourself you want to look like "xxx".

It's funny how we have someone we look up to and tell ourselves we want to emulate.

This can work against us because the other person could be way off from what we could ever look like.

I have no hips, and if I wanted to look like a curvaceous vixen, I would disappoint myself every time.

I choose to love my 'no hips' form.

4 – Change your look from time to time, just to keep things fun.

Ever come across someone who still has the same hairstyle since the 80s?

It's like they think they only look good as their younger self.

Changing up your hairstyle and look can allow you to accept yourself under any condition.

Wear a different kind of outfit or color your hair.

Don't like the new haircut?

Hair grows back.

Learn to rock any style you experiment with.

This can cause you to be more flexible and flow with any changes in your life.

5 – Rock what you got.

Stop waiting to look a certain way before you can love yourself for who you are.

If you are overweight, then love every ounce of you as you attempt to be healthier.

If you are wrinkly, love those wrinkles and enjoy your skin for how it has carried you through life.

6 – Go to the gym to ACTUALLY train, not to show off the latest style in workout gear.

It seems like women have gotten more attached to their style than their training.

Go to the gym in a T-shirt and sweats, and train your butt off.

Stop going to the gym to seek out attention, or compare your body with someone else's.

You may be in better shape now than the other chick, but honor her journey as much as you want other people to honor yours.

CHAPTER 8
MANAGE STRESS

"The day she let go of the things that were weighing her down, was the day she began to shine the brightest"
-Katrina Mayer

"I have to get the kids to 3 separate schools, make sure I packed all their lunches, find clients to work with, manage the clients, make sure all the kids do their homework, pick up the house and keep it in order, make sure I keep myself in shape, make dinner, clean up, show up as a seductress to my husband (mate) and get some sleep.

Uggggggghhhhhhhhh!!! I am SOOO stressed out!!!"

Sound familiar?

- What kind of stress do you have in your life? What is your breaking point? How do you deal with stress?
- Do you internalize your stress?
- Do you know how to release stress?

Unmanaged stress is a sure way to quickly age a person, especially if you internalize the stress.

Stress can show up in the face.

Stress can show up in poor posture.

Stress can show up as a lack of sleep.

Stress can show up in the breakdown of relationships.

Stress can show up as disease in the body.

It's crazy how stress is pushed aside like it is the ordinary sign of the times.

We live in a fast-paced world and you just gotta learn how to deal with stress.

Go outside and smoke a cigarette. After work, go get a beer.

Really?

Do you really think putting poison in your body is a solution to dealing with stress?

If you don't learn how to release stress, you will battle through life and age rapidly.

WE NEED A WAKE UP CALL!

HOW UNMANAGED STRESS ROBS US OF OUR PERSONAL POWER

STRESS KILLS because we aren't taught how to properly manage it.

Go to the doctor, tell them you are depressed, and they will give you a pill.

Now that's a way to help you gain personal power...NOT!

Instead of asking questions about what is going on in your life and perhaps investing a bit more time with each patient, doctors are taught to "medicate" rather than investigate.

Recently, while on vacation with my husband, we were relaxing by the pool.

Next to us was a man continually speaking on the phone about how stressed out he was.

He was speaking loudly, interrupting everyone's peace while all of us were attempting to relax at the pool.

He kept saying things like,

"I am at the pool and I am so stressed because I have so much to do, but I love it."

Instead of realizing how he was ruining everyone else's vacation time, he wanted to make sure the person on the phone and everyone around him knew he thrived on stress.

This man was overweight and looked aged beyond belief, yet he keeps telling himself he thrives on stress.

How can anyone age productively when they continually live on stress and won't allow themselves to relax and detach?

Unmanaged stress brings unneeded high levels of cortisol in your body, which unproductively ages you fast.

We are living in a "quick fix" society.

We must deal with something as fast as possible so we can move on to the next thing.

Because we look to fix things quickly with the least amount of effort, we are losing our power.

Funny enough, there is a reason why we tend to value anything we have applied effort towards.

It's like our blood, sweat, and tears into acquiring something allows us to value the attainment of said goal/item.

Value YOU by investing into yourself.

Power is built from maneuvering through the challenges of life and going through them with courage. This power allows us to strengthen our body, mind, and soul.

A wonderful example of this is from "The Parable of the Butterfly"[3]:

---

3 https://clockworxnz.wordpress.com/2016/07/28/the-parable-of-the-butterfly/

"One day while walking through his garden, a man found a chrysalis hanging delicately from a branch.

As he admired it, it started to move and a small opening appeared.

The man enchanted, watched for hours as the Chrysalis moved frantically, the butterfly struggling to free itself from its confinement through the small opening.

Then almost suddenly the butterfly stopped, appearing as if it had gotten as far as it could go and could go no further.

The man, feeling sorry for it, decided to help the butterfly, and with a small knife he gently slit open the chrysalis, allowing the butterfly to emerge easily.

The butterfly broke free, only to wilt over in a completely motionless state in his hand. Its tiny swollen body and shriveled wings withered and deformed.

The man continued to watch expectantly, waiting for the moment the wings would unfurl, expand and enlarge enough to support the still limp body, enabling the butterfly to get up, but he waited in vain.

Instead the butterfly spent the remainder of its short existence crawling awkwardly, dragging its fragile body and shriveled wings, and never able to fly.

What the man in his kindness, goodwill and haste failed to understand was this:

The restrictive chrysalis and the struggle required for the butterfly to get through the small opening is nature's way of forcing the fluid from the swollen body into its wings.

The wings can then unfold enabling the butterfly to fly and achieve freedom."

> **"We need struggles in our lives, if life would not contain obstacles it would cripple us. We would not be as strong as we could have been and would never be able to fly." - Author Unknown.**

Individual true strength and power comes from learning how to maneuver through the challenges of life.

Bottling up emotions and attempting to "act" as if all is OK only blocks energy in your body.

You know when you are not being honest with yourself, and your body weakens with lies.

EMBRACING AND RELEASING ANY STRESS YOU HAVE BOTTLED UP INSIDE OF YOU

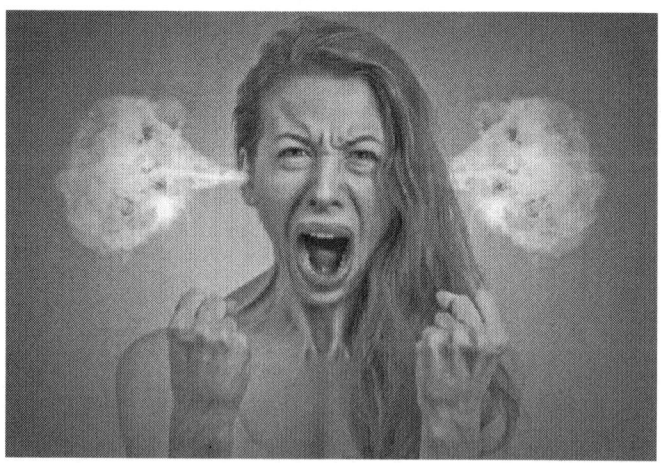

Ever heard the following expression?

> **"It's not what happens to you, but how you react to it that matters." – Epictetus**

I would like to add something to this quote: "It matters how effectively you release it."

MANAGE STRESS

Have you ever had clogged plumbing?

The more gunk you allow to stay stuck in the pipe, the more backed up it becomes.

If the clog is not cleared, then water cannot move freely through the pipe.

Your unmanaged stress can become like the gunk in the clogged pipe.

Deal with and release your stress to unclog the energy in your body.

Whether you realize it or not, you have a patterned behavior in dealing with stress.

Some people blow up and yell at other people around them when they are stressed.

Some people will close down and not talk when stressed.

Some people will talk more (and talk nervously).

Often times, we won't even know we are acting a certain way because it is an ingrained behavior we have conditioned ourselves to carry out.

Want to know how you deal with stress?

Pay attention to how you show up when you feel pressured.

If you hold stress in, then practice with ways to release it.

You will know this by the way you feel.

You will feel off, or feel like you are "faking" how you feel.

You may have a knot in your throat for not wanting to express how you feel.

Only you can shift your behavior.

A good therapist can help, but ultimately you must be willing to do the work.

Remember what Jesus (Yeshua) said in the Bible: "Tend the Garden" which can be interpreted as "do the work".

If you react with stress – meaning you lash out at others, yell, cry, or get nervous – then look for productive ways to release the stress.

Unproductive ways of releasing stress can cause breakdowns in relationships, bringing additional stress into your life and making you look much older than you actually are.

Unreleased stress can cause one to lose sleep.

Sleep is extremely important as we age. Sleep is when your body regenerates itself and heals.

If you are dealing with insomnia or have issues with sleep, then most likely you are not releasing stress.

There were times when I would wake up to use the bathroom and then go back to bed, only to have my mind keep me awake for the rest of the night.

My mind would be replaying made-up scenarios in my head.

I would scare myself beyond reason, and then not be able to sleep.

The next day would be horrible because my mind was in an all-out war, attempting to put me in full protection/fear mode.

I would be running around, 'trying' to keep it all together from an exterior perspective, yet internally I just wanted to crawl in bed and hide from the world and my responsibilities.

Whether you realize it or not, unreleased stress shows up in our face and body posture.

Look at people when you are walking around outside or at work.

Can you tell the ones who don't handle stress well from the ones who do?

Of course you can!

It is absolutely evident.

Yet, we walk around thinking we are Oscar Award winning actresses and no one can tell how stressed we are.

Even if no one can tell how stressed you are, your body knows.

Your body is attempting to work in overdrive while putting out messages to "PROTECT, PROTECT".

Those messages of fear going through your body are not allowing your body to function correctly.

You have high levels of cortisol running through your body.

This is why people develop ulcers or stomach issues: They cannot properly handle stress.

Don't be like some of our younger women, who think they have to be in their 'safe zone' to operate productively.

Although stress can show up in our bodies negatively if not handled correctly, stress is actually good for us when we learn how to handle it (Reread the butterfly story I shared with you earlier. The struggle is how the butterfly develops its wings).

The gift is in the struggle (or as my husband likes to say, 'The gift is in the shit'). There is an opportunity for growth in every negative occurrence.

It is up to you to recognize and acknowledge it.

Get comfortable with being uncomfortable, and you will age effectively.

💡 TIPS FOR CRACKING THE CODE: MANAGE STRESS

1 – Lots going on at work? Create a checklist and go through each item from the most urgent to the least urgent.

Stay focused while at work.

You are at work to work and provide a service, not to socialize or check all your social media sites.

Be as productive as possible while at work so you can leave knowing you gave your best.

2 – Stop doing so much for your kids.

Teach your children how to be more independent.

Allow them to make their own lunches.

Make sure they are holding themselves accountable to getting their homework done.

Teach them how to cook so they can make dinner for the family from time to time.

Give them chores around the house.

Not doing things for them does NOT mean you don't love them.

Of course, give them love, time and attention, but don't hover over them.

Being a micro-managing "helicopter" parent is how many children grow up without the ability to productively handle stress and daily challenges in their adult lives.

Some women find value only in their children, but at the expense of losing touch with who they are.

By all means, allow your children to deal with contrast.

Don't fix it all for them.

As hard as it is to see any of our kids suffer, it is important for them to learn how to deal with their own lives so they can be productive, independent adults.

3 – Do something for yourself.

Take a dance class, a yoga class…something that can help you detach from the stress of the day/week.

When we do not allow ourselves to set aside time to take care of ourselves, stress builds up because we believe there is never any time to do enjoyable things that are productive and healthy for ourselves.

4 – Dealing with something that is causing you to break down?

Step away from the situation for a few minutes and focus on your breathing.

Step outside of yourself and ask yourself the following questions:
- What can I control in this moment?
- What is absolutely out of my control in this moment?
- What is the solution to this situation? What COULD be a solution to this situation?
- What small action can I immediately take to start taking ownership of this situation?

Once you've answered all of the questions, bless the situation and sprinkle it with your magic.

Express gratitude for the opportunity to deal with the challenge in an empowering and positive way.

See it as another step towards becoming a strong, powerful and confident woman.

5 – Don't take anything personally.

People will have opinions and may not be very nice at times.

Feeding into their negativity or hatred won't help you.

Instead, it will only have you participating in the madness. Read the book "The 4 Agreements" for more help on this.

7 – Meditate or pray (more on that later)

Meditation and/or prayer have been proven in numerous studies to do wonderful things for reducing your stress levels, among several other health benefits.

Further ahead in the book, I'm going to show you my personal approach to meditation and teach you how you can modify it for your own personal benefit.

CHAPTER 9
GRATITUDE & APPRECIATION

"Gratitude turns what we have into enough"
-Melody Beattie

Gratitude and appreciation are key for aging gracefully.

Being grateful to be YOU allows you to know you are enough.

Ever meet someone who worries or complains all the time?

The older they get, the more miserable they seem and look.

The lines from their worries and complaining are well imbedded in their face.

On the flipside, when you are grateful, your whole being is energized and your face brightens up.

We live in the most comfortable and abundant times in history, yet more and more people are ungrateful.

Why?

Because survival requires less effort and many people have grown entitled.

"I deserve to have this now!"

We want what we want now.

We have grown impatient with inconvenience.

This attitude is causing us to become more and more ungrateful for the simple things.

Being more and more ungrateful for the simple things is causing you to age faster.

Stop and think for a second:

- Do you have running water?
- Do you have a bed to sleep in?
- Do you have food to eat?
- Do you have money in your bank account to pay your rent and bills?

These are all things we need to survive, yet every day we take them for granted when needed.

Ever have the electricity go out, causing you to figure out how to adapt?

Although it's inconvenient to live without electricity, it causes us to move beyond our normal way of being.

It has become increasingly easier to look at what we don't have and take for granted what we do have.

If you were to stop and actually write down what you are grateful for in your life, I would be willing to bet that you have LOTS to be grateful for.

If you don't think you do, it's because you have trained yourself to be ungrateful.

CHOOSING TO FOCUS ON THE POSITIVES, NO MATTER THE CIRCUMSTANCES

Do you ever find yourself saying these things in your head (or out loud):

- *"Why does this always happen to me?"*
- *"My life sucks"*
- *"No one likes me"*
- *"I have been by myself my whole life"*

Can you imagine YEARS of asking yourself these questions?

It's like you are mentally beating yourself up.

Do you really think you will age productively while tearing yourself down?

Let's put it this way: Have you ever associated with women who are ungrateful?

They are horrible to be around and can suck the life out of you.

They want to drag you down with them.

They are like "crabs in a bucket".

Have you ever seen multiple crabs in a bucket?

When one attempts to crawl out, the others pull the one attempting to crawl out back into the bucket.

Women who are miserable will commiserate together and pull you into "the bucket" with them.

These are the women who gather to speak about all the wrong their partners do, or they spread the latest gossip.

Underneath it all, these women are emotionally miserable and project their misery onto those closest to them.

Projecting their misery allows them to take the focus off themselves and place it onto someone else.

Gossip in any form is unproductive for anyone and does not benefit your mind or body.

I recently dealt in a transaction where the buyers were attorneys.

Being an attorney can come with multiple downfalls.

You see the worst of people.

You are taught how to prove someone else is wrong. It can shine a light on the negative in the world.

This particular couple looked for anything and everything they could find to be offended about.

They compiled "evidence" after "evidence" to support their case, saying things like "other people cannot be trusted and do not have my best interests at heart".

It made what could have been an enjoyable experience into an experience of feeling like "teeth were being pulled" for all of us involved in the transaction.

I have often wondered if people who look at all the bad in the world can truly appreciate the beauty in the world.

When everyone and everything is evil, how can you feel safe or see beauty all around you?

On the contrary, have you ever been around a person who expressed gratitude to people?

These people are great to be around.

They have a 'light' that brightens the room.

Their smile is infectious.

These people are generous.

They look at what they have, rather than what they don't have.

Grateful people live in the present moment. THIS MOMENT RIGHT NOW.

It's hard to be ungrateful when you are living in the present moment.

> **You are not attempting to predict the future and relive the past. You embrace this moment for you are living, knowing it could be your last.**

Gratitude is like a magic potion for aging effectively.

The energy associated with feelings of gratitude and appreciation is truly life-enhancing.

Being in a state of appreciation raises the levels of oxytocin in your body, which improves your ability to love yourself and others.

How could that not be productive?

Test it out for yourself.

Every day, look for things to appreciate about you and your life.

Anytime your mind wants to focus on all your wrinkles or sagging skin, shift the thought to something you like about yourself.

See how you feel after doing this for a minimum of 30 days.

CONSTANT COMPLAINING DISCONNECTS YOU FROM APPRECIATING THE JOY OF LIFE

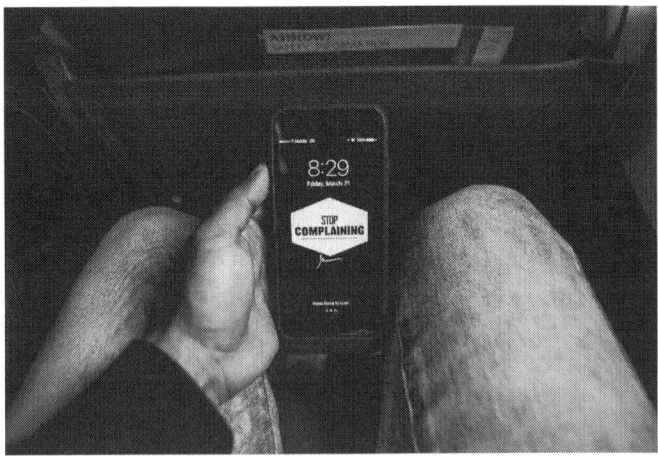

Having an ungrateful heart is the fastest way to age someone.

These are the people who look 60, yet are only 45 years old.

For these people, it's always about what they don't have, rather than appreciating what they do have.

GRATITUDE & APPRECIATION

A sure sign of ungratefulness is complaining.

Complaining has become more and more prevalent in our world.

Just look how popular the major reviewing sites have become!

"If you don't treat me with respect, then I will post a negative review about you and/or your company."

Interestingly enough, the people who are easily irritated are the ones who would take the time to complain about something.

I understand these sites have value, but like anything else, some people take advantage of having a voice.

Nowadays, most people won't even wait patiently in a line at the market before they start complaining.

People HATE waiting. It is such an inconvenience.

"Don't you know where I have to be?" We protect our spot like it's our first-born child.

Is it really that important? Is it really going to hurt you to allow someone to "cut" in front of you?

Driving in traffic can truly test your level of gratitude and appreciation.

Have someone cut you off and let the gratitude start spewing from your mouth as your hands throw up gestures of love!

It will take practice, day in and day out, to strengthen your gratitude muscles.

You are where you are because you have trained yourself to be this way.

If you are accustomed to constant complaining, then do your best to stop yourself in the moment.

Want to know how you show up to other people? Ask them for honest feedback.

Social media gives everyone a voice, especially the complainers.

Post something and watch how many people can attack you for your views.

It becomes an outright war about opinions.

Friendships can be lost over arguments on social media.

Who is right and who is wrong?

An opinion is just that: An opinion.

We say we have freedom of speech, yet you can say something to hurt someone's feelings and the end result is catastrophic.

The simple remedy for this is to allow people to be who they are. When you come from a place of gratitude and appreciation, it is difficult for anyone to offend you.

With eyes of appreciation, any moment can be one to show gratitude and appreciation for.

GRATITUDE IS THE REAL SECRET TO LIFELONG HEALTH AND HAPPINESS

When I met my husband, he was angry at life and women.

He went through a bitter divorce, lost his children and his job, and was not a happy person.

He blamed everyone else around him.

On our first date, I remember how he described his life in about 30-40 minutes and talked about how victimized he felt.

He didn't hold back.

When he was done, he said "Ok, that's enough about me. Tell me about you."

I spoke about myself and my life, and was done in about 10 minutes.

When I was done, he said "Wow, you are happy." I said, "Yes, I am happy."

He was surprised that I could actually BE happy. I was and am happy.

Being grateful for the triumphs and tragedies in your life allows you to be happy. True happiness is the key to true youthfulness.

With great power comes great responsibility.

We are all powerful beings.

Most have forgotten this power and simply exist for the sake of existing.

This is why it has become so easy for people to be ungrateful.

Getting comfortable with your power will allow you to become more grateful.

This power will fuel your appreciation for life.

And with this power comes a state of innocence.

An innocence of the creative little girl you once were before the pain of life tainted you.

Keep the innocence of the little girl you once were, and look at the world with those innocent eyes.

As a child, your imagination allowed you to see the best in the world.

It is all still there, but your vision has simply become clouded. Don't let "reality" shine brighter than your perception.

You get to call the shots.

Begin to explore more of who you are, rather than allowing society to dictate who you need to be.

GRATITUDE & APPRECIATION

Society will never be happy with who you are, so stop attempting to please society.

Start being you for YOU.

As you begin to become more comfortable with being yourself, start looking at how amazing your life is.

When you come from a place of gratitude, it becomes easy to see the beauty within and without. Life becomes a gift, rather than a chore.

Being grateful allows you to accept others for who they are and not expect them to change for you.

The beauty of this world is its diversity.

If we were all the same, it would be boring.

Embrace the differences as much as you are inclined to embrace the similarities.

Women do not have to be judgmental and condemning.

We do not have to demean others to make ourselves look better.

We can look for the best in others and build other women up.

We can appreciate the beauty in other people, even the younger ones.

We were all younger at one time.

Like I said before, let's cooperate and stop competing with each other.

Honor all people's journey as much as your own.

💡 TIPS FOR CRACKING THE CODE: GRATITUDE AND APPRECIATION

1 - Invest time in the morning to be grateful. Even if it is only 10 minutes.

Sit down and write out what you are grateful for.

I like to buy the inexpensive Composition Book notebooks and write out my gratitude list.

When I write it out, I allow myself to feel grateful for the life I have.

Strive to write down at least 5 things every day, and stick with the habit for at least 30 days.

Just for fun, see if you can come up with new things every day instead of repeating the items from the previous day! ;)

2 - Stop complaining.

You didn't get your favorite parking spot?

Tell yourself there must be a better one for you, or perhaps recognize it as an opportunity to walk farther and get some exercise.

If you have a habit of complaining, ask people you care about to point out if you are complaining to see if others perceive you as a chronic complainer.

Realize and KNOW that for every negative occurrence in your life, there is an equal or greater benefit lying ahead.

I got that from the book "Think and Grow Rich", and it has helped me SO much!

3 - Play "The Perfect Game".

My mentor Matthew Ferry shared this simple exercise with me, and it has been such a game changer in helping me become more appreciative of the things I have in my life.

Here's how it goes[4]:

"Whatever is offered, you take it. Whatever is suggested, you do it. Whatever happens, you laugh and you declare it perfect."

This doesn't mean you take drugs when offered, or blindly say "yes" to every sales pitch that comes your way.

It simply means you open yourself up to all of the potential opportunities coming your way, even if they don't seem like opportunities at first.

Didn't get the dream job you wanted?

PERFECT! Know there is a reason why you didn't get the job, and that there must be something better coming your way.

4 - When Jay and I first met, I would play "The GLAP Game" with him.

GLAP stands for "Good Luck, Abundance and Prosperity".

Whenever we would go somewhere and something cool would happen (no matter how small), I would say something like, *"Ooooh, this is such a GLAP moment. GLAP follows us wherever we go".*

It was such a fun way for us to play with life.

It had us laughing and smiling so much, all while strengthening our gratitude muscles.

---

[4] https://blog.matthewferry.com/just-say-yes/

5 - Call someone you care about (or talk to them in person), and let them know how grateful you are for having them in your life.

Be open and honest with them.

Hug them if you can.

Focus on how their positive qualities and presence in your life has helped you become a better person.

Be present in this moment with them.

These moments can crack the code of aging so effectively and actually energize your body.

6 - Do you feel like you are already grateful and show appreciation?

If you do, yet you look at others like, *"Mary is just so ungrateful, she has no idea how to be grateful like me",* then stop putting yourself on a pedestal.

Allow other people to be who they are.

Offer advice only when someone asks for it.

You are not the ruler of the universe.

You know your body.

Live in it and allow others to get to know theirs and live in their own body.

CHAPTER 10

ARE YOU MAKING YOURSELF OLDER & SICKER?

"You can't help getting older, but you don't have to get old"
–George Burns

I've started off each chapter with a favorite quote of mine, but this chapter needs TWO quotes…

*"We don't stop playing because we get old;
we grow old because we stop playing"*
–George Bernard Shaw

Why do we convince ourselves we are old?

Who cares if our numeric "birthday" shows 60, or 70 or older? We don't have to be anything until we decide to be something.

Yes, our bodies are changing and we will show signs of aging, but who said we have to BE old?

"Being" old only makes you older.

Your spirit and vitality can be 25, even while your physical body is 80.

Stop believing what society tells you about "getting old" as a woman.

This is your life, so start writing the story of how it will evolve.

Don't depend on others to write your story for you.

Remind yourself of your strengths, no matter what age you are.

If you are 60 years old and still weight train like a beast, then pat yourself on the back.

Acknowledge all you can do and build yourself up.

Give the best attention to yourself when you are being and acting healthy, especially as you get older (and make sure to do the same for others).

Set incentives for being in great health, but do NOT set incentives for yourself when you get sick or feel weak.

Don't expect people to coddle you.

Don't baby others when they get sick or attempt to act weak.

NOTE: I am not saying to kick someone when they are down. Of course, if someone needs help, then having compassion is a gift.

I have a daughter who likes to "act" like she cannot do something so someone else can do it for her.

Kids are smart.

They understand that they can get more attention when they are sick or weak.

Sadly, this pattern of behavior continues as we get older.

"Cough cough...I'm sick, take me to the doctor, help me feel better".

We are losing our power and strength because it's so easy to be weak.

FOCUS ON "SELF CARE" INSTEAD OF "SICK CARE" FOR BETTER HEALTH AND VITALITY

More people are addicted to health care to feel better than ever before, simply because they truly believe it is needed.

If you watch TV or listen to the radio, we are bombarded with messages of "Speak to your health care professional to see if this is right for you".

Doctors are becoming a crutch for the elderly because most people have no idea who they are or how to be healthy.

The medical industry rewards us for being sick through prescription medication, which can become highly addictive.

Knowing what pills to take and when to take them can be one of the biggest challenges of getting older.

Look at most people who are 70 years or older – they can take 10 or more pills PER DAY.

It seems like the older we get, the more we depend on a pill to make sure we are healthy.

The only one who wins in this scenario is the pharmaceutical industry, aka BIG PHARMA.

What would happen if people were cut off from their prescription medications?

We would first have anarchy, or societal unrest.

Which would then lead to some form of revolution!

Depending solely on your doctor to keep you in good health is absurd, if not outright delusional.

YOU MUST get to know your body first and foremost.

Know when you feel off.

You are the one who is living in this body for a lifetime.

Why not get in tune with what works for your body and what doesn't?

Most people won't invest the time to get to know their own body because they are too busy or too comfortable.

Yet the moment they are diagnosed with a life-threatening illness, they want to do all they can to get healthy so they don't die.

And don't get me wrong, there are doctors who can definitely help one get better.

However, doctors do make mistakes.

It is virtually impossible for one doctor not to make any mistakes.

It is sadly inevitable for it to happen.

Someone will eventually become the result of some kind of medical mishap.

Will it be you, or a loved one?

It won't be you if you begin to take care of yourself NOW.

It doesn't matter what age you are.

You can make the decision to honor your body and spirit by truly knowing who you are.

There will be times when working with a medical professional will be necessary.

But through knowing YOU better than anyone else, you can feel confident in trusting what is right for you.

If you are diagnosed with a life-threatening illness, know your options.

Simply following a doctor's advice without getting a second opinion or trusting what is right for you is not honoring you or your body.

Don't expect your doctor to heal you from the effects of aging when you have negative ingrained beliefs and have neglected your own body for years.

Want to age effectively?

Know what is best for you and practice being youthful.

Too many of us are convinced we are old.

Too many of us are easily swayed by what we are told by medical professionals.

A diagnosis can be given to a patient who believes EVERYTHING their doctor says.

The patient then places so much value on the diagnosis coming from their doctor that they deteriorate fast (even if it was a false diagnosis).

A patient can give up and lose all hope.

Once hope is lost, your strength to live diminishes.

There are numerous cases of people who were given a false diagnosis, yet died thinking the "death sentence" was accurate.

Know yourself no matter what information is given to you.

This will allow you to determine your state of mind and take full control of your well-being.

AGING WELL IS A STATE OF MIND

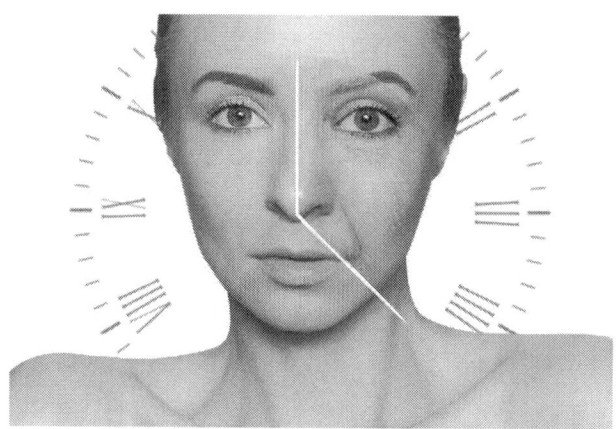

On top of living a healthy lifestyle, aging effectively comes down to your inner spirit.

I've met so many women in their 60s or beyond who think, *"I can't wear this because I am too old!"*

Well, says WHO?!

I recall being in my late 30s and looking in my closet, thinking to myself *"I won't ever be able to wear this sexy dress again because I am getting close to my 40s, so I better give it away."*

I laugh when I think about how I thought back then.

I thought turning 40 meant the end of any potential sexiness in my life.

Little did I know that I would gradually grow to love and accept myself more as I got older.

Fortunately, I now have a husband who buys me plenty of sexy clothing for us both to enjoy.

If you convince yourself you are old, unattractive, not worthy, or boring, then you will be.

I LOVE seeing older women (or men) strutting their sexy selves proudly.

The world may not always approve, but when done with dignity and respect, you are honoring yourself.

You are as old as you think you are.

This is your life. You call the shots.

You already know, no matter what you do, you will die one day.

Do you want the process to be filled with sickness and sadness, or do you want it filled with good health and happiness?

ARE YOU MAKING YOURSELF OLDER & SICKER?

It really is your choice. It begins by the cumulative choices you make, day in and day out.

If you continue to work as you get older, then have fun with working.

Don't view it as a struggle.

View it as life-enhancing.

Anything you do can be done with a purpose.

We don't have to look for THE purpose, because you ARE the purpose.

You can bring purpose with you to anything you do, bringing the life back into your years.

People will work in horrible jobs that break them down, looking forward to retirement and thinking this arbitrarily-chosen time period is when they will truly live.

They finally retire, only to get sick and die just after retirement.

Why?

Because they have been poisoning their bodies everyday with the attitude they brought to their job for years.

By the time they retire, their bodies are shot and they have no idea how to handle actually being at peace.

Some lose meaning.

Some lose direction.

Some lose purpose.

It is way too uncomfortable and scary. Plus, now they are OLD. OLD is so scary, isn't it?

It doesn't have to be.

THE ELLEN LANGER EXPERIMENT

Harvard psychologist Ellen Langer performed a well-known experiment in 1981 with 8 men in their 70s.

These men were taken to a converted monastery in New Hampshire.

Some of these men suffered from arthritis and some even walked with canes.

As part of the experiment, Ellen Langer and her crew had the monastery look like a place from 1959.

This was their "home" for 5 days.

The men were directed to live as if it were 1959, to be who they were back in 1959.

They were even treated as if they were their once younger selves.

They were responsible to carry their items up the stairs and handle their own business.

The men had conversations about "current" events as if it were the late 50s.

There were no mirrors to remind the men of how they presently looked.

They dressed as if it were the late 50s.

Interestingly enough, at the end of the 5 days, the men were tested and all of them improved from when they had entered the converted monastery.

The men looked younger, were able to move better and some even had improved vision!

The men believed they were younger and their bodies followed suit.

They improved so much that they played a spontaneous game of "touch football" while waiting for the bus.

For more information on this study, search "What if Age is Nothing but a Mind Set?" in the New York Times Magazine[5].

This was a powerful study reminding all of us how we are making ourselves old and sick.

Change your mindset on your age and change your body.

You'll be pleasantly surprised with what happens. ;)

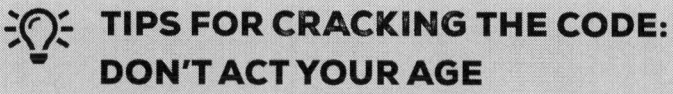

TIPS FOR CRACKING THE CODE: DON'T ACT YOUR AGE

1 - Wear lingerie. Wear it for yourself.

You don't have to walk around the house with it on (unless you and your mate feel comfortable with it), but wear it under your clothing. Feel sexy and BE sexy because you are!

2 - If you are accustomed to wearing conservative clothing, spice it up a bit.

Wear something out that is totally NOT you.

Walk around with it on, and do so with pride.

Other people's opinion don't matter. Your opinion is the only one that matters. Rock it, girl!

3 - Buy a wig and wear it out with your sassy outfit, or just wear it with something you would normally wear.

Put on a different persona.

Pretend to be someone you are, not just for the fun of it.

---

5 https://www.nytimes.com/2014/10/26/magazine/what-if-age-is-nothing-but-a-mind-set.html

You can be a sexy vixen or a librarian. You call it.

4 - Go dancing.

Who cares what kind of dancing? Just go out and dance. Don't dance for anyone else but yourself.

Years ago, I signed up for pole dancing lessons.

I loved this class because the instructor would remind us each time, *"You are not dancing for anyone. You are dancing for yourself. Close your eyes and feel the music."*

This was so powerful for me because for the first time in my life, I felt like I could really dance!

(Funny story: Everyone always made fun of my "white girl" dance for the first 40 years of my life)

5 - Anytime your mind wants to remind you how old you are, remind yourself how beautifully young you are.

It doesn't mean you are NOT going to tell people your age.

Age is a number, and resisting the act of telling your age only causes you to think you are old.

Our age is actually made up at the end of the day, because we made up the calendar that dictates it, so just have fun with it!

6 - Go back in time.

Dress the way you did when you were younger.

Listen to the music you listened to back then.

Pretend you are in your younger skin.

Do this for as long as you can get away with it (without watching TV or listening to the radio from today's times).

CHAPTER 11
SILENCE & SOLITUDE

"Come into the silence of solitude and the vibration there will talk to you through the voice of God"
-Paramahansa Yogananda

I'd like to start this chapter off by quoting an excerpt from "Life and Teaching of the Masters of the Far East" by Baird T. Spalding:

"Still in the Silence

Yet in this complete silence there exists God's Greatest Activity.

Again, I am undisturbed and complete silence is all about me.

Now the radiance of this light spreads to God's vast universe and everywhere I know there is God's conscious life.

Again, I say fearlessly, I am God; I am silent and unafraid."

I read this one day and it helped me realize how important silence is.

This is when we can listen with our heart.

The silence is when your inner knowing (a.k.a. God) speaks, and if you are in solitude, it is easier to hear.

I think the monks have it right with being in solitude.

This is when they can have a true connection with the divine.

Your body is a vessel to carry you through this life.

Your true essence lives in this vessel for a short time until your body expires.

If you listen in the stillness, you can listen to what is most loving and productive for you.

SILENCE IS YOUR BEST FRIEND AND MOST TRUSTED ADVISOR

What is the longest amount of time you have ever allowed yourself to be silent in solitude?

Most people have no idea how to be in solitude.

We surround ourselves with constant noise.

When we are by ourselves, our mind begins attacking us about all we have to do, almost to the point where most people prefer not to be by themselves or sit in silence.

Stop reading and pay attention to what is going on around you.

Even if you are in a room by yourself, there is probably a buzz or some sort of noise.

Almost all homes have at least one TV inside.

Wtih our cell phones, most people are walking around with their face in front of a screen and headphones in their ears.

It is rare for any of us to have actual silence, which has made most of us uncomfortable with silence.

Years ago, I participated in a self-help mastery course where one of the assignments was to be in a tent by myself (in the middle of nowhere) for 24 hours.

These 24 hours could be spent in any manner I chose, except absolutely NO SPEAKING was allowed and I was all by myself.

We were only given a small snack to eat if we got hungry, some water and a journal.

At the beginning, I wasn't really sure what I should do aside from journaling.

I had so many questions about the direction my life was heading.

But there is only so much journaling you can do within a 24-hour period before one gets bored (at least I did).

Then the voices attempt to get louder.

Paying attention to where my mind was going had me all over the place.

It truly was a profound time for me as it was the first time I had ever been alone with my thoughts for that long.

During this time of solitude and silence, I found out more about my mind and how it attempts to protect me.

Think about what you could accomplish if you would allow yourself time to be silent and in solitude. Not only could you create a plan, you could also visualize and feel what this would be like to you.

Living life in the real world can make it challenging to have silence and solitude because we can be pulled in so many directions.

Being pulled in so many different directions can cause one to feel agitated and scattered.

If you are a mom, it is most likely rare for you to have any time to be in solitude, much less in silence.

Silence can be found in the early morning before anyone gets up, and only if you are able to get up before everyone else.

Once the kids get up, "solitude" time most likely does not exist.

If you are in a relationship, solitude can be even more challenging because your mate wants attention too.

All these people around us get a piece of us, but we rarely give ourselves time to simply BE.

Fortunately, you don't have to take a vow of silence to crack the "Fountain of Youth" code.

MAKING SOLITUDE A DAILY RITUAL IN YOUR SCHEDULE

Simply set time aside to be in solitude or silence.

Invest time to NOT answer phones or emails.

Invest time to detach from what others expect of you. Invest time to BE present to you.

Being in solitude can be scary for lots of people, as this leaves you alone with your own thoughts.

Although we like to think we control our thoughts and we are own best friend, our thoughts can feel like an outright attack at times.

The more your mind is out of control, the more fear-based your thoughts are.

Fear can cause added stress in your body, causing you to age faster.

The more you practice solitude, the better you will become at controlling your thoughts.

Most of us don't ever invest time to stop and simply be with ourselves (and by ourselves).

This often causes us to feel like our lives are spiraling out of control.

Although we live in some of the most comfortable times in recorded human history, there are many more cases of depression and loneliness.

And while we are more comfortable, we are not more aware.

Many women would rather be their depression/anxiety instead of sitting in silence/solitude (which brings them value).

Perhaps being depressed or anxious makes you feel valued because you get to see your therapist, or you get a prescription for a drug that relaxes you.

**Solitude/silence can bring awareness.
Awareness brings peace.**

Train your children to be OK in silence and solitude, without a screen in front of their eyes.

In today's times, we are teaching our children how to become robots more than human beings.

Teach your children about going within and being present in the moment.

They learn by our actions and not by our words, so start by doing it yourself.

Silence can bring such a great sense of inner peace to your being.

Your being will be strengthened, allowing you to age effectively.

Plus, you will start to learn how to trust yourself because you will know what KNOWING feels like.

💡 TIPS FOR CRACKING THE CODE: SILENCE & SOLITUDE

1 - Do a technology fast.

Start with a day.

No TV, no phone, no computer.

This is a good way to start, which can lead you into a day of solitude.

Depending on your circumstances, you may even choose to have certain parts of the week where you abstain from using any form of technology whatsoever.

2 - Practice letting other people speak.

While they speak, you listen.

Actually listen to what they are saying and dig a bit deeper to find out more about them.

See how it feels to get out of your own head and actually listen to someone else.

You'll be surprised to see yourself better able to engage in conversations and get to the core of what people really want.

Don't forget that we have two ears and one mouth for a reason!

3 - Take a walk with no phone or headphones.

Actually be present on your walk.

Smile at other people but don't talk.

See if you can connect with your eyes or smile.

So often, we tend to use our music and headphones as a way to distract ourselves from having to deal with the world around us.

Instead, embrace your present surroundings and take in everything using your five senses.

4 - Get up an hour earlier than you normally do.

If it is in the early morning before anyone else is awake, then sit and focus on your breath.

Pay attention to how it feels to simply focus on your breath.

Feel the life force energy flowing through you.

Do this for as long or as short as you feel inclined.

Enjoy the time that you have all to yourself.

Be grateful for the opportunity to simply be with yourself without any internal or external distractions.

CHAPTER 12

MINDFULNESS, MEDITATION & PRAYER

"Only a life of prayer and meditation will render a vessel ready for the master's use."
−George Muller

In cracking the "Fountain of Youth" code for your own body, it's important to realize you are more than simply your body.

There is a beautiful "energy" creating life in you.

Sit still for a minute or two.

Listen.

Look around.

Feel the energy within and around you.

Some call this "the God within".

Some call it "Spirit".

Whatever you call it, it is more than your physical body.

I will call it "the spirit within".

This is harder for left-brained people to grasp.

Left-brainers think with their minds, not their hearts.

They are analytical and love to look at facts and figures.

These people are great with charts and numbers.

But since they don't understand the "feeling" part of being human, they can discount this energy within looking for "scientific proof".

Sadly, most left-brained people have convinced themselves they cannot meditate.

Think of this section as strengthening your heart (a.k.a. coming from the heart).

It is more of an analogy, if anything else.

I have found this perspective makes "feeling" easier to understand conceptually, since this is more of a 'feely' topic (pun intended).

Investing time in the spirit found within allows you to strengthen yourself at your core being.

People who exist day to day without strengthening their heart and/or inner spirit often feel lost and/or not valued.

This can lead to feelings of hopelessness, depression, anxiety, moodiness, anger, sadness, despair, and more.

Your vessel (i.e. your physical body) will run better when you fuel it with meditation, mindfulness and prayer.

Want to look and feel younger?

This chapter is KEY!

HOW TO BE MINDFUL IN A BUSY, HYPER-ACTIVE WORLD

The definition of Mindfulness per the Cambridge Dictionary is[6]:

The practice of being aware of your body, mind, and feelings in the present moment, thought to create a feeling of calm.

I live in California and life is go, go, go.

---

6 https://dictionary.cambridge.org/dictionary/english/mindfulness

With 5 kids between Jay and I, our focus on our businesses, and the people who depend on us day in and day out, our lives can get pretty hectic.

I am amazed at how we keep going all day.

Truthfully, being mindful has allowed me to be at peace during hectic times.

When my 3 children were younger, life was super busy.

I was the one who did most things for my family.

Normally, I sacrificed time for myself.

I would wake up from 4-4:30 in the morning just to get what I wanted accomplished.

By the end of most days, I was spent.

I would just collapse.

I recall one day looking at myself in the mirror and asking myself, "Is this the way you want to live the rest of your life?"

There were many factors I was questioning that day, from a failed marriage to who I was as a human being.

I knew I had to make significant changes in my life if I was going to simply survive.

Those times were all about survival for me.

It is hard to thrive when you can't even survive.

I had to stop saying yes to doing it all for everyone.

It was time for me to look at how I could fill my tank while being better for myself.

At the time of writing this book, my bonus girls (my husband's biological kids) Alex and Gabbi are 9 and 11 years old.

When they were little, I chose to do too much for them.

I noticed they were expecting me to do it all for them.

I took a step back and realized rather than helping them, I was hurting them.

Doing too much for our kids teaches them nothing.

Allowing them to be responsible for themselves, on the other hand, teaches them personal power.

Now, Alex and Gabbi make their own breakfast and lunch for school in the morning.

They do their own laundry and are responsible for their schedules.

This allows me to invest time in myself.

I go outside and am mindful.

I sit down, I ground myself and simply "be" for a few minutes.

I pay attention to the beauty around me.

The birds are waking up and singing for me (at least this is what I tell myself because it helps me feel better).

I pay attention to how the wind moves the leaves and my inner spirit is speaking to me.

It is SUCH a beautiful part of my day.

I absolutely cherish this time.

It allows me to show up in a better mood with a wonderful foundation to my day.

You can even choose to be mindful as you are taking a walk.

Pay attention to the beauty around you.

Focus on your breath as you walk and look at the blessings which surround you.

Make sure to turn your phone off, or put it on "vibrate" to avoid distractions.

When my mom was alive, she would tell me that when a hummingbird comes close to you, a loved one is telling you they are near.

When I go out for my mindfulness part of the day, I set an intention to sense my mom.

Lo and behold, a hummingbird will make an appearance and I sense her love.

These moments can bring a tear of joy to my eyes.

It allows me to sense more to this life than what I can see with my eyes.

There is true power in mindfulness.

Don't make so many rules around mindfulness.

Simply be present to the moment.

You don't have to brag or tell people about your mindfulness routine.

This is your 'you' time.

Allow yourself to do it for you, not because you want other people to know how spiritual you are.

SETTING THE RECORD STRAIGHT ABOUT THE PRACTICE OF MEDITATION

What are your beliefs around meditation?

If your beliefs have stopped you from meditating, then redefine how you look at meditation.

Meditation is a great way to get out of your head and simply be present.

When I began meditating, my husband at the time (ex-husband) would condemn me because he would say I was allowing the devil to come into my mind.

Back then, I would hide while meditating.

It was not fun because although I wanted to detach, I also did not want him to find me and lecture me about how dangerous meditation was.

If you believe meditation is not "safe" for you, then perhaps pray.

Meditation can be as simple as closing your eyes and focusing on your breath.

As you inhale through your nose, hold it, and then release through your mouth or nose for 3 breaths.

It doesn't have to be for 1, 2, 3, or more hours unless you choose it to be.

When I began meditating, I would use guided meditations to help me get out of my own head.

I had a hard time quieting my mind.

The guided meditations would help me move beyond my mind chatter.

There are so many great guided meditations.

Go on YouTube and type in the kind of meditation you are seeking.

There are meditations for manifesting, being at peace, finding your ideal mate, bringing good health to yourself, being sexual/sensual, and the list goes on.

I have even used meditations to put myself in a restful state when I didn't sleep well the night before.

There are lots of good ones.

Just listen to it first and see if it resonates with you.

Then go to a place where you won't be disturbed and get into a different world.

It feels SO good.

If you are a pro at meditating, then you know what to do and all you gotta do is do it.

Schedule the time and allow yourself to enjoy the experience.

I have found that when people make it a "have to", they no longer focus on the value of meditating.

It becomes a chore and something to "check off" their schedule.

Do it simply because it is a part of you and feels good!

Honor your time to meditate and know this is a beautiful part of your journey.

Be flexible with how your meditation evolves.

The right way to meditate is the way that allows you to feel at peace and centered.

Stop telling yourself you can't meditate.

We all can.

You simply have to retrain yourself to be able to meditate.

You can even do a walking meditation, focusing on your breath as you walk around, paying attention to the beauty around you.

As you walk, smile with your breath.

View with your heart (without judgement) and come from a place of appreciation.

PRAYER WORKS FOR ANYONE, REGARDLESS OF THEIR RELIGIOUS BELIEFS

There is power in prayer.

For the sake of this chapter, let's view prayer as a way of speaking to your higher power, not a "want list".

Let's think of it as a way of releasing control over to your higher power.

Many times, when we are in pain or feeling less than, a prayer will set us at ease.

Holding onto the angst of a situation or problem and thinking you have to fix it can cause added stress.

Talk to God and let God know what you are going through.

Look at prayer as a way of sharing your struggles and asking for a solution.

Many people feel alone, with no one to really trust.

But with the power of prayer, you are not alone.

Prayer can also be a prayer of gratitude.

Want a relationship?

Start giving thanks for the perfect relationship and partner for you.

Want more money?

Start giving thanks for the abundance in your life.

In some of the darkest times of my life, I have gotten on my knees and prayed.

When my mom died, it was one of the most challenging times in my life.

My family and I weren't on good terms at the time and she was in a coma for over 10 days.

The whole experience felt like torture.

I prayed and prayed for peace, for my mom, and for my family who was struggling with the loss of my mom.

Prayer allowed me to survive.

If you are fortunate enough to have a partner you can pray with, then do it.

There is true strength in coming together with someone you love and seeking guidance, protection, gratitude, and love.

When you tell someone you will pray for them, actually pray for them.

It seems so cliché to say, "I will pray for you" and then forget to pray for them.

Stop for a moment and pray for their recovery, or for their strength.

See them as whole.

See them through eyes of love.

Follow through with your word so you can know the power of prayer.

You don't have to feel guilty when you are praying.

Guilt brings fear and condemnation, which breaks you down.

I was raised Catholic, and guilt was a huge part of my upbringing.

If you did wrong, then you were obligated to go to confession and pray to God for forgiveness.

I would get my 10 "Our Father's" and 10 "Hail Mary's" to pray to God, giving me a clean slate for the next time I screwed up.

Then of course, I would screw up again and feel guilty for screwing up again.

If you are Catholic and this is how you roll, then just realize the whole guilt thing does nothing for you except bring poison into your body.

Release guilt and feel free.

PLEASE know that I am not here to convert you to any religion.

Your beliefs are your beliefs.

The intent of this chapter is to remind you to connect to your higher power (i.e. God) and get out of your head.

💡 TIPS FOR CRACKING THE CODE: MINDFULNESS, MEDITATION & PRAYER

1 - Practice seeing people and yourself as healthy, whole and complete.

Don't bring pity or judgement to people.

Remember: What you give out is what you will get.

Pray for people in the same way you would want to be prayed for.

2 - Schedule time first thing in the morning to be mindful and journal if you can.

I enjoy going into nature and paying attention to the beauty around me.

You can sit, or you can go for a walk.

I won't give you a length for time, as time depends on you.

Flow and go with it.

I find this exercise serves me best when I don't assign arbitrary time limits to it or map out a specific route to walk along.

3 - Keep a prayer journal.

Journal about how you would like to improve, and what you need help and guidance with.

Pay attention to the answers you may get throughout your day.

I personally like to use good old-fashioned paper and pen because it really allows me to connect with my thoughts.

Plus, by relying on my own mind to come up with the answers, my intuition is more crystal-clear.

4 - Meditate at least once daily.

Start with making it short.

If you think you have to meditate for an hour every day, then it will be harder to meditate.

Go with 5 minutes at the beginning and gradually work your way up to 20 minutes.

Eventually, your life can be a walking meditation where you allow yourself to be at peace.

Meditation done once a day can do wonders for looking and feeling younger.

5 - Before bed, journal, meditate and/or pray to get yourself right before you go to sleep.

From personal experience, I get the most out of things like meditation, praying and journaling when I do them twice a day.

First thing in the morning, and last thing at night before I go to bed.

Doing these things before bed helps me to achieve a deep, restful sleep.

This leaves me feeling energized and alive when I wake up in the morning.

CHAPTER 13
HEAL FROM WITHIN

"The natural healing force within each of us is the greatest force in getting well"

−Hippocrates

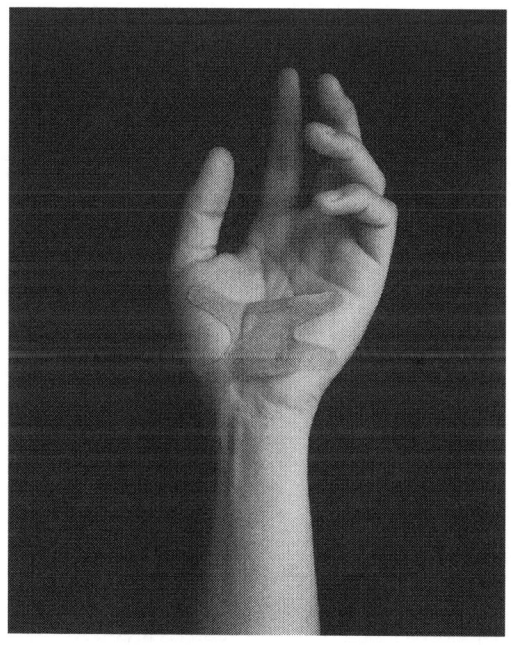

Have you ever sat still, paused, and observed life?

If you haven't, sit outside sometime (maybe a park, your backyard, or front porch) and simply observe.

Don't speak.

Simply listen.

Do you hear the little voice within?

There is an energy within you.

I like to call it "the God within".

Do you sense it?

If you don't, then it is because you are attempting to listen with your ears.

You must listen with your heart.

Listen with your being.

There is SO much more to you than your physical being.

There is so much more to this world than our eyes allow us to see.

Your mind attempts to protect you, and may even scare you.

When you work with your mind as a tool, rather than as an enemy, it can help you.

Your mind wants you to think you are only your body.

This is how your mind normally lives.

In an attempt to protect you, most times your normal mind will instill fear and prevent your true self from shining through.

At one time in my life, I had no idea I could actually control the thoughts in my head.

When I was a little girl, I prayed God would stop the "chatter" going on in my head.

I felt like my head was out to get me.

I was essentially scared of my own shadow.

I feared death and all that came with it.

I thought that all of a sudden, I would no longer exist and I would be voided from existence.

Today, I know this to be false.

I know there is life beyond this physical form.

While we are here in our bodies, it is important to take care of them (i.e. our vessel).

Part of taking care of your vessel is learning how to harness the power to heal from within.

TAPPING INTO YOUR OWN HEALING POWER

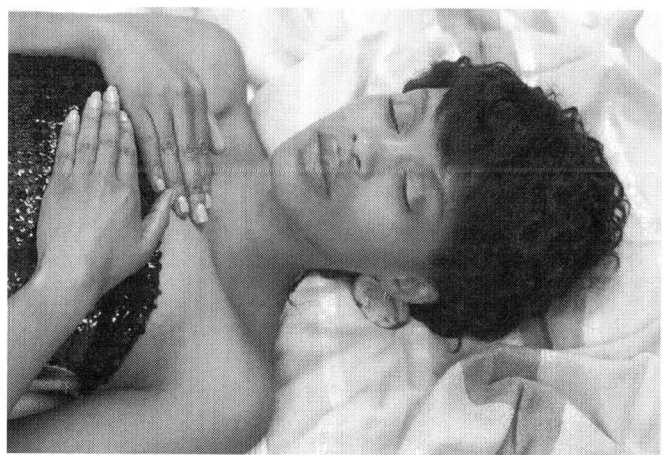

Most of us are not taught about our own power within.

We are taught to search externally for answers.

If you are sick, go to the doctor.

Are we ever taught about this power within?

Let's look at some written words from the world's wisest people providing this evidence:

1 Corinthians 3:16

Do you know that you are a temple of God and that the Spirit of God dwells in you?

2 Timothy 1:14

Guard, through the Holy Spirit that dwells in us, the treasure which has been entrusted to you.

Lao Tzu

Let it be still, and it will gradually become clear.

Buddha

Don't look for God in the sky; search His presence within your heart.

Swami Vivekananda

You cannot believe in God until you believe in yourself.

John Lennon

You're just left with yourself all the time. Whatever you do anyway, you've got to get down to your own God in your own temple. It's all down to you mate.

Edward Cayce

Know that all healing forces are within not without! The applications from without are merely to create within a coordinating mental and spiritual force.

Hippocrates

The natural healing force within each of us is the greatest force in getting well.

We have true power within us.

We have the power to tear ourselves down or build ourselves up.

Without realizing it, we are directing this power daily.

It can be through our self-defeating thoughts or through eyes of love. You get to decide.

This power within can shift a life-threatening illness into a miraculous healing.

You decide whether a life-threatening illness will be the reason you leave this physical form.

It can begin from the moment we are given news by a medical professional that we have a few months to live.

We have a choice to give up or gather every ounce of strength we have to live.

If you choose to live, you can use this news as a way to create a second chance at life.

At times and even without knowing, you will dig deep within to uncover a power foreign to your once "normal" self.

There is no giving up or giving in.

You have found hope to live and the decision is made to live.

This power is your God within.

This power is your healer.

Unfortunately, many take the "Western medicine" route and tear their bodies apart through chemotherapy/radiation, insane amounts of drugs, and risky surgeries.

These remedies kill the healthy cells, often times causing more harm than good.

Let's think about the human body for a second.

When you cut your skin, what happens?

It will eventually close up and heal.

Your body heals itself!

If you pick at your scar and don't allow it to heal, it can get worse.

In some cases, disease works in a similar fashion.

We have a wound that begins in our body (a disease), and we can discount it or get more stressed out about it.

We begin picking at it and making it bigger, causing it to get infected (i.e. unhealed emotional wounds).

Over time, with continual picking and irritation, the wound grows even larger.

By the time it becomes a serious disease, the wound has gotten out of control.

We then feel helpless, like there is nothing we can do.

We lose our power, and for some, hope is completely gone.

Knowing your power allows you to know and be comfortable with your own power to heal.

The power to heal is within all of us, and it is stronger than any of us allow.

For the most part, women are nurturing healers.

When our children are sick, we tend to them and help them feel better.

Yet when we feel off, we often push it aside and avoid taking care of ourselves.

This is a habit that must be broken.

It is time to get in touch with your inner healing power.

Want to know how to harness it more?

Practice getting comfortable with your power.

Practice healing yourself in the little things to help you know you can deal with the big things.

Let me be clear:

Am I saying not to ever use doctors or medicine?

NO!

I am saying you can get some additional ammunition (power) in your arsenal by tapping into YOUR PERSONAL HEALING POWER!

THE HEALING POWER OF UPLIFTING, POSITIVE THINKING

It starts with convincing yourself you are healthy.

"But wait! I have cancer, lupus, or some other disease, how can I possibly be healthy?"

Think of the disease as feedback from your body about what you have been feeding it, mentally and/or physically.

You MUST begin to give your body and your mind different messages.

Messages of health and love.

You are NOT your disease or sickness.

Love your body while you are experiencing illness.

Appreciate it for the feedback it is giving you.

Remind it what it is like to be fully healthy, whole and complete.

Remember: Thoughts are energy.

Energy travels. Positive energy heals.

Think about the power of prayer.

The power of prayer is a positive energy flow toward a certain outcome.

During your time of healing, do what you can to focus on uplifting thoughts, events and actions.

Watch funny movies, think happy thoughts, pray, or simply do anything uplifting.

Stay away from anything disempowering (energy vampires, stress, guilt, fear, television shows, etc.).

If you aren't allergic to flowers, smell fresh flowers and absorb their fragrant smell.

Picture the flowers bringing healing energy to your body.

Anything and everything you do during this time of healing will indeed heal you because you are convinced it will heal you.

Who cares if you are making it up?

You get to decide whether or not you believe it.

If you can convince yourself to believe it, then you are on the road to healing.

The more you "flex" your healing muscles, the stronger they will become.

This comes over time as you give your mind more evidence of your body's healing capabilities.

As your mind starts to know healing, as evidenced by feeling better or decreased tumor size, you begin to experience the healing power within.

If you are taking medication, declare it as aiding your healing power.

Ever heard of the placebo effect[7]?

The placebo effect works because the patient believes the sugar pill they're taking is a specific kind of medication or treatment used to heal their ailment.

This is simply another definition of our own innate power to heal ourselves, but we dismiss it because it is outside the norm of our understanding.

We are taught that all healing comes from the outside.

Even way back in the day, there were shaman healers who would heal people first (internally) before people would heal themselves (externally).

---

7 https://www.webmd.com/pain-management/what-is-the-placebo-effect#1

We MUST learn how to train ourselves to know our own healing power to heal from within.

Many people are caught up in the Western medical care system.

Due to this conditioning, it will take LOTS of training to think otherwise.

I am not suggesting to not follow your doctor's instructions.

I am asking you to trust yourself.

If you trust your doctor more than you trust yourself, you can harm yourself by this way of being.

To give yourself evidence you have the capacity to heal, practice affirming it.

I am suggesting you learn how to fully trust yourself in all things.

TIPS FOR CRACKING THE CODE: HEALING WITHIN

1 - Close your eyes and picture a mental laboratory.

You decide what this lab looks like.

Make it as simple or as elaborate as you like.

As you create what this lab looks like, picture the exterior and interior of this lab.

You will have 1-3 workers in this lab (don't make too many, because then you will focus too much on the workers, rather than the work at hand).

The purpose of this lab is to run your body in the manner you decide.

This lab will have any concoction you can create to heal your body from within.

You can mix it anyway you like, and you have access to anything you can create in your mind to help you.

You can create your own medicine (salts, creams, etc.) to be sent or placed anywhere in your body.

If a certain part of your body needs extra attention, then focus your healing attention here.

If you have a tumor in your uterus, have your workers work on erasing the tumor.

Instruct them to sprinkle it with love and light to properly eradicate it.

This is not going to be a one-time 'visualization'.

Think of this exercise as a form of light ray therapy.

You can do this in addition to any treatment you are getting from your doctor.

If you are getting treatment from your doctor, perhaps infuse this treatment with extra blessings of positive energy.

Remember: You are defining anything you do to your body as having a positive impact on its healing.

I have done this with some areas to release excess stubborn body fat.

I picture my little lab workers tugging and pulling in certain areas, sealing it to firm up my tummy area.

It's pretty cool to come from a place of power where you are designing your body, rather than feeling like you are helpless to change.

(NOTE: *This won't work if you don't exercise and eat like crap.*

Your mind will know you aren't taking care of it anyway because you haven't been working on your body and/or feeding it proper fuel.)

2 - Practice blessing your body.

If you are sick, then bless your body and sickness.

Look at the sickness as feedback.

What could this mean?

Should you get more rest?

Should you love yourself more?

Should you release resentment?

Bless the experience.

We are all energy, so sending yourself blessed energy is an uplifting experience.

3 - Do your best to not take any medication when you get something small like a headache.

Perhaps practice some slow deep breathing and surround yourself with love.

Do a healing meditation

The more you practice healing the little things when you don't feel well, the more you will trust yourself to heal the bigger things.

This may seem frightening at first, but if you trust in the process, you'll be pleasantly surprised by the results!

4 - When you get hurt, be at peace.

Look for solutions and see yourself as whole and complete.

Let go of your attachment to the pain.

Breathe through it.

I tell my kids when they get hurt (believe me when I say they don't like it), "That's awesome you can feel that, it means you're alive because if you were dead, then you wouldn't feel it".

5 - Mentally smile with parts of your body.

Close your eyes and smile into your brain, your eyes, your mouth, your neck, etc.

Imagine yourself sending thoughts of positivity and joy to the specific body part.

FEEL every last sensation in that body part and allow yourself to embrace the sensations.

When we are more in tune with our body, we start to grow appreciation for all the wonderful ways in which it serves us.

6 - As you go to sleep, mentally scan your body.

Send yourself healing white (or green) light.

Picture your body as the perfect body of health.

Send the light to parts of your body you feel require extra attention.

If it helps, visualize the light going from the top of your head and travelling through your body towards the body part you have in your mind.

7 - Picture healing energy in your hands.

Fill this energy with love.

As you relax, or before you go to bed, place your hands on parts of your body bothering you.

Feel the love transferring from your hands to the part of your body bothering you.

Be at peace and feel the love running through your body.

8 - Add something different to your healing within.

Pretend you are providing your own internal laser therapy and internally shoot this laser to parts of your face where you want to eliminate wrinkles or damaged skin.

Focus the laser on this area and see it magically heal and repair itself.

For me, the key to this is not looking at your skin right away and asking "Did it help?"

Act as if it helped and appreciate the treatment.

As time passes, keep appreciating your skin and see how this impacts your skin.

9 - Speak to your cells.

Tell them what you want them to do.

Thank them for regenerating and doing what is necessary to age effectively.

Express gratitude towards your cells for their remarkable ability to create such profound changes in your body at your command.

10 - Sending healing energy to others.

Close your eyes and think of someone who has been sick.

If they have stomach issues, then picture them and send their stomach loving energy.

Visualize this energy wrapping their stomach and healing them.

11. When you get up in the morning, say something like this:

> *Good Morning Beautiful (your name), I love you.*
>
> *I love who you are and who you are becoming.*

I am so grateful for my healthy and whole body. I am so grateful for the restful sleep that helps my body rejuvenate, rebuild, and heal itself.

I am happy, healthy, wealthy, wise, beautiful, sexy, powerful, empowered, radiant and strong. On this day, I commit to taking full responsibility for my wonderful life.

From this moment, I allow myself to feel vibrant, alive, and aligned with my truth.

I breathe and sense the wonderful energy pulsing through my body.

My blood flows through my body easily and effortlessly.

Today, I look forward to thriving with the amazing energy I have exuding from my body.

I accept the light that I am, and commit to shining bright for myself and others.

I am young, youthful and get younger every day.

As I sleep, my body easily regenerates new cells to create my perfect body of health.

Each of my cells work and cooperate together, keeping my body younger and more youthful.

I love myself and am a full expression of love to others.

My being represents pure joy and my presence is a gift to all.

I am a powerful manifester, manifesting all my desires easily and effortlessly.

It is so much fun to create my life from this powerful perspective, knowing all works out as intended.

Thank you for allowing me to share love with myself and others while fully participating in this journey of life.

I pay attention to the beauty in and around me, and show kindness to others.

Thank you for my beautiful life, thank you for my beautiful family.

Thank you for the ability to participate in life.

I love you (your name).

Let's go have some fun today!

CHAPTER 14
THE POWER OF TOUCH

"Touch seems to be as essential as sunlight"
-Diane Ackerman

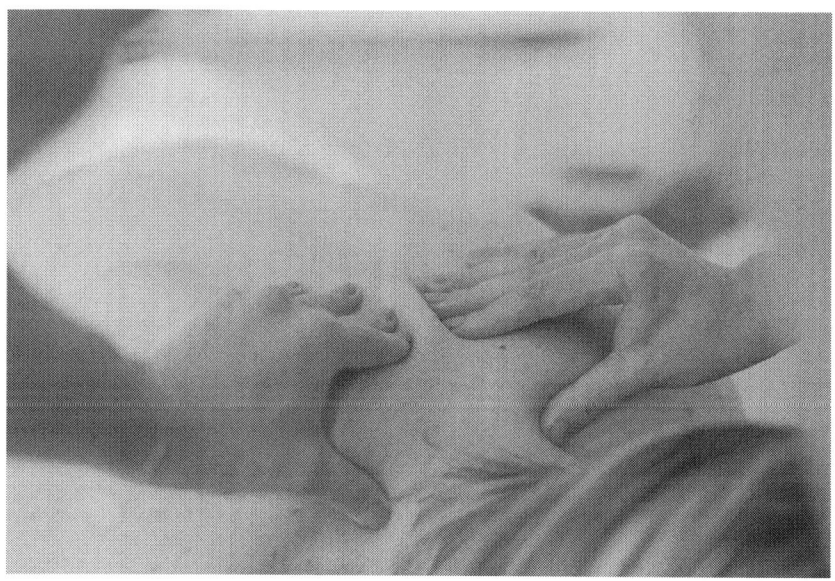

There is great power in touch.

Even newborn babies understand this power.

Newborn babies flourish when held.

If babies are left apart from their mothers or not held, they do not flourish.

As we get older, the power of touch becomes increasingly powerful.

Yet, we dismiss the power of touch, thinking we must strive to "get ahead" as there is just too much to do.

Have you been adjusted by a good chiropractor?

What a difference it can make in aligning your body!

Have you gotten acupuncture?

This can help with pain management and stress relief.

Do you ever allow yourself to get a good massage?

Massage has been found to have healing properties and can help remove fascial adhesions.

Have you ever allowed someone to sit and play with your hair?

It feels so good to have someone run their fingers through your hair, to fix your hair up, or even to simply massage your scalp.

The thought of a wonderful scalp massage is so exhilarating!

Stop what you are doing for a second and close your eyes.

Give yourself a quick scalp massage.

Feel your fingers run across your scalp and even play with your hair.

Doesn't it feel so good?

The examples mentioned above are some of the ways that others can touch you.

TOUCHING YOURSELF, AND OTHERS TOO

What about you?

How often do you touch yourself?

I am not referring to masturbation.

I am referring to touching yourself in loving ways.

Many times, when I feel stressed, I will give myself a neck massage and feel the energy from my hands transferring to my aching neck.

Touching myself allows me to know the power of my own touch.

Have you ever felt the energy coming from you skin?

The warmth of this energy can feel so good and soothing,

How about with your kids or your partner?

When was the last time you touched them to show love and affection?

Do you hug your partner or children before you leave one another?

Or do you hurry off because you are in a rush?

When I met my now-husband, the moment we embraced, I could feel the energy from his heart.

Now, when I am stressed or simply want some extra love, I ask him for a hug and all is well in my world for that moment.

Even while in bed, if he wraps his arms around me, I feel safe and loved.

Most of us will discount our own touch or the touch of our loved ones.

Many have gotten closer to their pets.

Pets love unconditionally and don't give us comments about what feels good or what doesn't.

Some people have come to prefer relationships with their pets more than a relationship with a human being!

Pets are easy to love because they are loyal, and people can let us down.

Love your pets!

But be careful with putting all your energy into your pet.

Being a complete pet lover can cause you to lose touch with reality.

Interact with other people as often as you can, even if it is by simply shaking their hand.

Many people nowadays have become germophobic.

"Oh no, I need my antibacterial gel to make sure I don't get their germs."

I am not recommending you go around touching everyone, but I am recommending you stop being afraid of life.

As my husband (who is a huge student of quantum physics) often says,

"You always get what you focus on".

If you become afraid to interact or touch other people for fear of germs, then you will easily attract germs.

Just so you know, germs are everywhere.

Your own skin has all sorts of bugs and germs.

As you become more in touch with your beautiful power, you will begin to realize touching others is simply a way of sharing affection.

See this as such.

There is no need to become paranoid that this person is carrying germs or will get you sick.

Looking for evidence to get you sick will get you sick.

Begin to embrace life and people.

TIPS FOR CRACKING THE CODE: THE POWER OF TOUCH

1 - Massage:

There are many forms of therapeutic massage.

ART, Cranial Sacral, Deep Tissue are all amazing for when you are feeling stressed.

You can even give yourself a quick massage.

You know the pressure you like best, so get at it!

Practice giving those you love a massage or rub down.

You will feel better for allowing them to relax, and they will feel more loved by you because you invested a little bit of time to show them you care.

2 - Chiropractic

We all need spinal alignment from time to time.

My husband and I know how important it is to maintain our back health and see our chiropractor weekly.

If you can go every week or at least every other week, do so.

This is WAY more important than your nail or hair appointment.

3 - Physical Touch

When you meet someone and you feel compelled to hug them, ask them if it is OK to give them a hug.

Not everyone is lovey-dovey.

It is important to respect how other people operate.

When you shake someone's hand, look at them in the eyes and don't give them a limp wrist.

Too many people these days don't even have life in their handshake.

When you wash your body, don't rush.

Enjoy touching your skin with your washcloth and enjoy the process of cleansing your skin.

CHAPTER 15
BREATHING

"When you own your breath, no one can steal your peace"
-Unknown

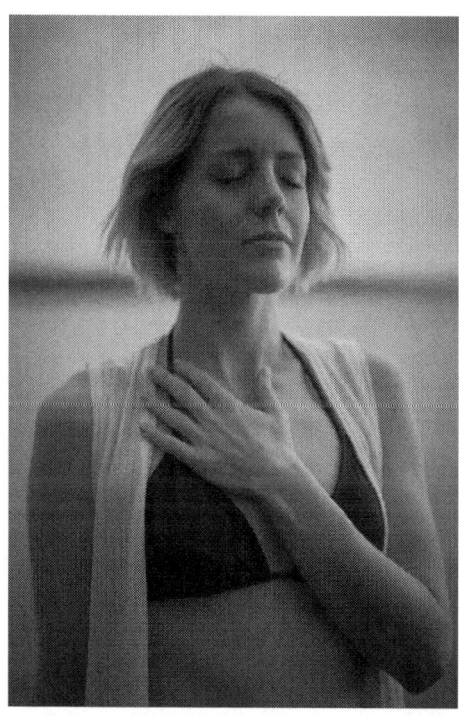

This Chapter was written by Dr. Mickra Hamilton. Enjoy!

We all have two things in common. Two things required for the human experience that are non-negotiable and not optional: We inhale when we are born, and exhale as we transition into death.

We take a breath the moment we leave the nurturing environment of our mother's womb and if we don't, we are promptly turned upside down and soundly swatted to ensure we make the journey all the way in.

We breathe, and breath is life.

While we often discuss the fact that we can live weeks without food and days without water, we seldom think of the reality that we have only minutes of life without breath.

It is understood that breath is central to life, and a key player in how we perceive our experience.

This fact often goes unacknowledged as we assume that breathing is an automatic process that is mainly outside our control.

It's time for some really exciting news!

We can consciously control our breath, and in doing so realign our body, mind and spirit in an effortless, integrated whole to promote youthful longevity and flawless aging.

In this chapter, we will look at the essential nature of breathing for health and wellbeing, aging, beauty and performance.

We shall discover the link between ancient breath practices and youthful aging, and the importance of renewing and refining these practices to assist with the sometimes less than kind environmental modern pressures that accelerate aging.

We will explore critical aspects of breath, heart and brain integration and the importance of creating optimal coherence in each of these systems.

Finally, we are going to discuss powerful strategies to leverage the epigenetics of breath and promote youthful longevity, vibrant health, flourishing well-being and flawless aging.

FROM THE ANCIENT TO THE MODERN

Ancient texts are filled with recommendations of the use of breath to modulate and influence the expression of body, mind and spirit.

Specifically, to maintain a joyful state of youth and cultivate a deeply connected and integrated state within and without.

The Chinese referred to the breath as "qi", the Hindus as "prana" and the Greeks as the "divine presence".

These cultures view breath as a "vital principle" that flows through the body as a kind of energy.

Many of us today know ourselves to be this vital principle and many others are on the verge of this self-discovery.

Today, we have many modern techniques that are rooted in the ancient and interconnected to the present through the science of what is actually happening in many of our human systems.

What was once in the lane of the mystical has now moved into the lane of the knowable.

Research into basic physiology and the effects of applying breath control strategies to integrate the body/mind/spirit complex lend credibility to the value of monitoring and regulating our breath to restore it to its once effortless and automatic state.

This is where epigenetics or how the interaction with the breath affects everything from consciousness, physiology, cognition and physical performance.

THE EPIGENETICS OF BREATH: BREATHING FOR HEALTH AND WELLBEING

Remember those environmental pressures I mentioned in the introduction above?

Well, we now have a strategy for action to create a new breath expression.

The game changing science of epigenetics (i.e. how our genes and environment interact) assists us to create personalized and precise optimization breath strategies to age flawlessly as we adapt and thrive under modern environmental pressures.

Every decision we make contributes to this process in some way.

The air we breathe and how we breath it, the food we eat, our quality of sleep, the cars we drive, the products we clean with and put on our skin, the thoughts we think, the levels of stress we carry and the chemicals/medications we dump into our water supply all have an effect.

The more we optimize and enhance ourselves, the more quickly we upgrade to flawless aging. It is, after all, an inside job waiting for us to be the change we want to create within us.

Modern environmental pressures and 24/7 access to a world of information and activity has created so many amazing opportunities to learn, grow, explore and experience adventure.

On the flip side, it has created a change in our natural breathing process that is affecting not only our health and wellbeing, but most importantly our opportunity to age flawlessly.

Additionally, chronic stress, processed foods, unhealthy indoor environments, lack of fitness and a disconnection from nature combine to create a perfect storm to ensure that aging is not a graceful process.

One of the fundamental challenges to flawless aging is a rarely identified issue: Chronic over-breathing.

We might ask, What? Is it possible that we can over-breathe similar to the way we might be "over served" at our favorite cocktail event or when we "over consume" those delicious chocolate brownies?

The answer is "yes, of course," over-breathing is possible and much more common than we think.

Let's explore this in greater detail.

Breathing is generally an involuntary activity that we engage in unconsciously and rarely think about, yet it is always there.

We have a common misperception that breathing in more air increases oxygen in the blood and it simply isn't true.

We can optimize the breath to move us towards thriving health, well-being and flawless aging.

Or, we can ignore it and pattern in all sorts of dysfunctional breathing behaviors.

These behaviors prime the system to go out of balance and alignment.

Generally, once breathing is out of sync, it stays there and we can spiral into poor health, age more rapidly and perceive the world through a limited lens.

Our breathing habits can make the difference between thriving energy, fresh youthful appearance with glowing skin and being a dried up, wrinkled old prune who looks as if she has had a hard life.

What is over-breathing?

What are the outcomes from over-breathing, and how do we know if and when we are doing it?

Over-breathing, also known in the medical world as hyperventilation, is when we eliminate more carbon dioxide (CO_2) than the body can produce.

This can happen when we breathe fast, take in too much air volume, and breathe in the chest as opposed to the diaphragm.

Excessive release of CO2 limits the body's ability to oxygenate the system, constricts blood vessels and leads to rise in blood pH along with reduced blood flow to the heart, brain and skin.

Common symptoms are anxiety, tingling in the lips, hands or feet, headache, lightheadedness, brain fog, poor sleep quality and fatigue.

Ladies, if you feel anxious, have cold hands and feet and always feel tired, over-breathing could be part of the issue.

Let's have a brief refresher.

We breathe in oxygen (O2) and breathe out CO2. We all know the importance of O2, but what about CO2?

Most of us have been taught to believe that CO2 is nothing more than a waste product and significantly less important.

In reality, CO2 is the key variable that allows the release of O2 from the red blood cells to be used by the body.

Simply put, the amount of CO2 in our blood cells determine how much oxygen can be delivered, so how we breathe determines how much oxygen we can use.

Great oxygen delivery to the skin assists with clearing toxins faster, creating more rapid cell turnover, sleeping more restfully and improving mood and performance.

Now that we know the importance of ideal O2 delivery and optimal CO2 balance, let's get practical and determine what is happening in our own individual breath.

Do we breathe in an ideal state, or have we created dysfunctional processes that have led to over breathing?

Let's take a look at a few essential key areas necessary to determine the current status of our breath and what we can do to optimize this essential system once identified.

These areas are rate, position and volume.

Today, the average woman breaths short, shallow and in the chest at a fast "breath per minute" rate.

What is the ideal breath rate per minute? Let's look historically to find both the answer and an alarming trend.

The average breath rate in 1929 was 5 breaths per minute, which is the ideal resonance breath rate of the heart, or the breath rate that keeps the system in homeostasis or balanced.

This rate has gradually increased each decade, and by the 1980s the breath rate averaged 12 breaths per minute.

Breath speed has continued to rise at an alarming rate, and today the average breath rate is approximately 18-24 breaths per minute.

While the finest medical institutions have determined normal breathing rates to be between 12-20 breaths per minute, we see that this is quite off from the ideal breath rate of 5-6 breaths per minute.

We might ask how has this happened with no one in the medical community paying attention.

Disease rates are skyrocketing, we are aging at unprecedented rates, people are sick and tired, sad and lonely, and many cannot glimpse much hope for a clear and simple way to return to their once vibrant state of well-being.

Fortunately, it can be as simple as slowing the breath speed.

How about the position of the breath?

Our natural breath process is to breath effortlessly through the nose with the mouth closed, drawing the breath gently down into the belly to breathe with the diaphragm.

This natural breath is generally effortless and silent, with very little chest movement and no tension in the chest, shoulders, neck and head.

The majority of people breathe through their mouths and predominantly from their chest.

This results in decreased nitric oxide production which is important for many essential body processes and also results in the diaphragm locking down from little to no use.

When this lock down leads to over-breathing, we have altered pH, increased inflammation, decreased immune system function, muscle soreness, lower back pain, poor sleep, chronic exhaustion and many more systemic effects.

When you train yourself to breathe diaphragmatically (or belly breathing), you remind the body of its natural breath, strengthen the most stabilizing central muscle in the body and send signals to the entire system that it is youthful and thriving!

What about volume, or the amount of air that we breathe in?

Our breathing capacity is six liters but a normal breath is half a liter.

Too much volume equals too much CO_2 elimination.

The problem is that when we take a deep breath we can inhale too much air and the result is "what goes in must come out."

"Take a deep breath."

This is a phrase we say and hear all the time, yet this ever-present mantra often does us more harm than good.

Our well-meaning cultural editors (parents, spouses, teachers, coaches, yoga instructors, etc.) have our best interests at heart as they advise us to take a deep breath.

They are simply trying to help us calm down because we experience heightened emotions, or we are in yoga class, birth preparation or in the gym in an intense workout.

Unfortunately, this well-meaning advice often leads to over-breathing.

Through proper regulation of the amount of air that we take in the body, we can fine tune our respiratory gases to activate clear thinking, a state of ease and performance not previously achievable.

Enough of the somewhat boring science!

Let's evaluate the breath to gauge our current state, gather enough personal data to create an individualized plan to optimize the breath, and create flawless aging.

Open the timer on your phone, place one hand on the chest and the other just above the naval.

Breathe in and note a few things.

- Is the breath through the mouth or through the nose?
- Is the breath shallow or deep?
- Fast or slow?
- Smooth or ragged?
- Silent or loud?

Once we have explored these questions and the qualities of breath have been determined, turn on the timer and count the number of breaths per minute.

When breathing effortlessly through the nose, into the belly at a slow yet gentle and silent rhythmic rate (5-8 breaths per minute), congratulations!

You have achieved an ideal breathing pattern.

If, however, we find ourselves breathing through the mouth with shallow upper chest movement, a faster rate of breathing and we can hear ourselves breathing, it will greatly benefit us to bring our full awareness to the breath process and begin a strategic process to optimize it immediately.

Our body will thank us for it with the reward of flawless aging.

💡 TIPS FOR CRACKING THE CODE: BREATHING

I'm going to give you some prescriptive breath strategies to elevate awareness and harness the magical power of the breath to live a beautiful, youthful and exciting life.

Breath work, or prescriptive breath techniques. have been used as a transformative tool since the beginning of recorded history. They assist us to become more centered and improve self-awareness of how we respond to life.

They are free, safe and easy to use. They serve as a powerful tool in our beauty kit to restore our system to a thriving and vibrant state.

Additionally, breath work promotes youthful aging, enhances performance, cognition and better quality of life, which all leads to a more pleasurable life.

Breath techniques influence both physiologic (by stimulating the parasympathetic nervous system) and psychological factors (by diverting attention from the thoughts).

Evidence-based research is quite robust and unequivocally validates that modifying our breath, especially in respect to slowing and relaxing the breathing rate while optimizing the breathing position diaphragmatically, has countless psychological and physiological benefits.

Every relaxation, meditative and calming technique, as well as performance enhancing strategies used today, relies on breathing.

It is the common denominator in all approaches to calming the body and aligning and integrating the body, mind and spirit.

With so many different strategies for breath work, how do we know where to begin, what type to use, and when?

Let's explore some easy quick win strategies.

Breath for Youthful Longevity and Flawless Aging

Regular diaphragmatic breathing exercises reduce stress and anxiety, regulate the body's pH and lower cortisol levels while improving mood, attention, focus, concentration and overall well-being. More importantly, it decreases the expression of aging and inflammation.

Breath for Relaxation

Box Breathing, or tactical breathing, was developed for the military special operations community to allow quick access to a calm, focused and centered state prior to or during a heightened stressful experience – five minutes is all that is needed.

- Get comfortable sitting or lying down
- Inhale gently and softly into the solar plexus (upper belly) for 4 seconds
- Hold the breath for 4 seconds
- Exhale gently for 4 seconds, letting the air leave the body
- Hold the breath for 4 seconds
- Repeat for up to five minutes or as long as necessary to get control of the body and mind.

The autogenic training method of relaxation based partly on slow and deep breathing (developed by German Scientist Johannes Heinrich Schultz) is one of the best-known breathing techniques for relaxation in the western culture.

Breath for Performance Enhancement

Ancient Breath Practices and Youthful Longevity

Pranayama is breath retention, i.e. holding the breath was a way to increase longevity

Coherent Breath, Heart & Brain Integration

Heart Math Coherent breathing

Trust me when I tell you how powerful the breath is as an instant tool to change your state of being.

When we optimize the breath, we align and integrate all our human systems, and move into a state of breath, heart, brain and mind coherence.

In this state, we know who and what we are, we know how we serve, and we know that we are free to explore this experience to our fullest capacity.

Cheers to ideal breathing and flawless aging!

It's crazy how we take our breathing for granted.

Many of us won't know what it is like to fully appreciate breath until it has been taken from us.

Ever almost drowned?

Coming up for breath after being under water can sure make one appreciate breath.

When you are stressed, ever pay attention to your breathing?

Stress can cause shortness of breath or cause you to have fast paced breathing, thereby making the stress feel more intense.

Your breath can be a barometer for how you feel.

BREATHING

Pay attention to how you are breathing and you will most likely be able to tell if you are stressed or at peace.

Your breath will be completely different.

The more you practice paying attention to your breath, the more of a master you will become at controlling your breath.

I honestly believe (no scientific proof to this) that part of the reason people enjoy smoking is because they are unconsciously focusing on their breath.

It slows down the pace of their breath and causes them to relax.

You take in a deep puff to inhale the smoke, then blow out the smoke in a full blow.

If you could do this without smoking, it would be a great way to calm yourself down after a hectic day.

Without even realizing it, most of us do not even know how to breathe correctly.

Proper breathing allows energy to flow through your body.

There is great power in your breath when controlled.

If you are still and pay attention to your breath when you take a deep breath in, then you can feel the breath traveling through your body.

I use my breath to give me strength while weight training.

It's crazy to see how many people hold their breath while attempting to lift weights.

Breathe and power out your breath while training.

You will find your training to be more intense and effective when controlling your breath along with your movements.

CHAPTER 16
GROUNDING

"If you want to lift your spirit, you have to ground your soul. That's why your 'sole' is on the bottom of your feet."
—Alexis Brooks

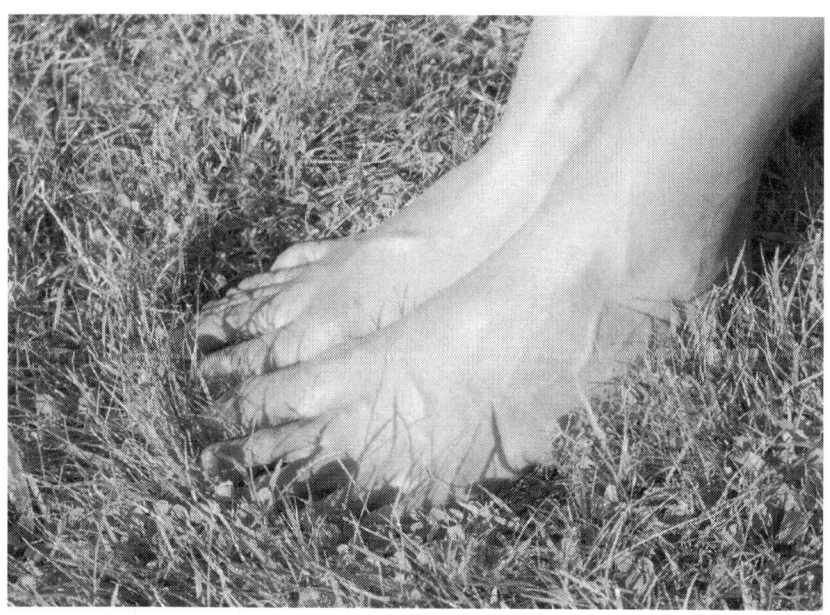

There is a reason the earth is called "mother".

Our Mother Earth has healing components we've gotten disconnected from.

In an attempt to make our lives more comfortable and convenient, we are losing touch with our Mother Earth.

Grounding (or earthing) is a way for us to reconnect with Mother Earth.

In earlier times, we would walk barefoot to get from place to place, or sleep on the ground.

Being connected to the Earth this way literally allowed our bodies to become energized.

The Earth is an electrical planet.

Our bodies also produce electricity, yet we can be thrown off by modern technology and our shoes.

Plus, we rarely ever place our bare feet on the grass or dirt.

Again, this is completely "disconnecting" us from our power.

Stop what you are doing for a couple of minutes and think.

When was the last time you placed your feet on the grass, walking along the sand on the beach or on dirt (and how long were your feet there)?

If you are like most people today, you rarely put your bare feet on the grass, sand, or dirt.

We think the dirt or grass is too dirty.

"I don't want sand in my car." "My feet will get dirty." "Ew, the dirt is gross."

We are inconveniencing ourselves out of great health with this attitude.

Certain cultures even think walking barefoot outside can make someone sick!

When I was a kid, we ran around barefoot on the grass, made mud pies and were actively playing outside.

With our technological advances, we are training our kids to get their playtime with screen time.

GROUNDING

There are apps to make it "seem" like you are in nature, and there are games to connect you with another part of the world.

Kids today have almost no direct exposure to Mother Earth.

Even PE time is getting cut short in school.

Plus, no one can run around barefoot because it is a liability.

In doing so, we are confining ourselves and children out of great health.

For a better explanation on grounding (or earthing), buy the book "Earthing, The Most Important Health Discovery Ever!" by Clinton Obrun, Stephen T. Sinatra, MD, and Martin Zucker.

Here are some excerpts from the book:

"Earthing is both a timeless practice and a modern discovery.

It simply means living in contact with the Earth's natural surface charge-being grounded – which naturally discharges and prevents chronic inflammation in the body.

This effect has massive health implications because of the strong link between chronic inflammation and virtually all chronic disease, including the diseases of aging, and the aging process itself."

"Throughout practically all of history, we humans have maintained a direct physical connection with the Earth -the skin of our bodies touching the skin of the Earth."

"We walked barefoot and slept directly on the ground.

We were at all times naturally charged with the healing energy of the Earth.

We wear nonconductive shoes with synthetic soles, walk on carpeted floors, and sleep in elevated beds.

We do not live on the ground.

We even live and work high off the ground, in high rises.

We rarely go barefoot outside."

"Consequently, our bodies have become chronically charged with inflammation, an unnatural development, and one that appears to represent an overlooked reason why immune dysfunction and inflammation-related health disorders have dramatically proliferated, ravaging adults and children alike.

We have lost our electrical roots, the Earth's electrical ground that serves as our primordial anti-inflammatory protection."

"Grounding is a simple way to get on the track of better health but it is not a cure all.

Don't expect to get healthy if you continue with unproductive habits (not exercising or eating well).

Sure, it can help you feel a bit better but to truly get benefits, ground while improving eating habits, exercising and working on your inner muscles."

Grounding is so simple and can be as easy as eating lunch outside on the grass with your bare feet on the grass.

Get comfortable with your "hippie" self and enjoy nature for better health.

My husband wrote about grounding in his book The TOT Bible (Ladies, if your husband isn't getting his hormones checked yearly, he should probably read it. I also have a chapter in there along with Dr Jim Meehan on women's hormone optimization therapy, a.k.a. HOT.)

Here is what my hubby had to say about grounding (earthing):

> If you suffer from chronic pain and neurological inflammation, I highly recommend you investigate **grounding** (also known as **earthing**).
>
> There are more than 20 peer reviewed studies on grounding demonstrating its profound effects on reducing inflammation.
>
> I recommend reading the deep analysis Ultimate Longevity provides on the profound research on grounding.
>
> If I were a doctor (which I am not), I would prescribe every human on planet Earth to a minimum of 30 minutes each day grounded in nature to be healthier.

💡 TIPS FOR CRACKING THE CODE: GROUNDING

1 – Carry flip flops in your car.

Stop whenever you can while driving and take a break.

Sit outside and get your feet planted on the dirt, grass or sand.

Enjoy a book or your food to reconnect with the Earth.

See if you can "feel" yourself being better connected with Mother Earth, and take note of how your mood and perspective on life rapidly changes.

2 – Buy a grounding mat for your bed, or to place your feet on while at the computer.

They really do work.

I bought one for my husband Jay for Christmas and our sleep has improved tremendously.

Aches and pains due to inflammation are often dramatically reduced if not eliminated completely.

Whenever Jay works from his studio office, not a day goes by where he doesn't spend a significant amount of time barefoot, standing on the mat to mimic the experience of grounding outside.

If you're looking for a good mat, I highly recommend getting one from Ultimate Longevity.

3 – Let your kids play outside on the grass/sand/dirt barefoot.

Give them time to play outside more often.

Get them away from the screens!

There's a good reason why the world's most powerful executives intentionally limit (or even prevent) their own kids from engaging with the same technology they sell to other people.

Don't get me wrong, technology is AMAZING and has allowed us to do many wonderful things.

But is has to be used as a tool for productivity and moderated in healthy fashion.

4 – Give yourself the opportunity to run and play barefoot outside.

Be OK with feeling the sand between your toes.

Sit on the grass.

Allow yourself to feel the sensations within your feet and your body as you touch the ground and move around.

It may seem odd at first, but soon you will find yourself profoundly connected with Mother Earth.

5 – Sunbathe in the nude

If you can sunbathe in the nude in your own backyard or somewhere you feel comfortable, then this is ideal.

This has nothing to do with sexuality, but rather to be able to lay your whole body on the earth and acquire the benefits of laying nude on the grass/dirt/sand.

If you haven't given it a try, try it. You never know, you might like it!

CHAPTER 17
WORK YOUR BODY

"The less we move, the less capable we are of moving"
–Pete Egoscue

Today, life is very comfortable.

We live in homes where at the touch of a button or the sound of a voice, something works for you.

Less and less effort is needed to actually accomplish something.

Think about how at one time, we hunted and worked to feed our families and keep them safe.

We were constantly moving.

Now, we have a dilemma.

When life becomes too comfortable or easy, how do we challenge ourselves?

It's definitely not by sitting in front of the TV for 3-5 hours a day.

It's not by sitting in a bar drinking for a few hours a night.

Time and time again, I hear statements like YOLO (You Only Live Once), which gives people permission to destroy their bodies.

The issue is that most people don't care or even pay attention to taking care of their body until they are diagnosed with a life-threatening illness (or they lose a limb).

THEN, people "wake up".

They value life.

Once someone values their life, they want to change their diet and implement a workout plan.

Unfortunately, for some it can be too late depending on how much damage has been done to the body/mind.

You have ONE body, RIGHT NOW.

This body was given to you through this lifetime.

How your journey evolves will be based upon the choices you make.

You may be handicapped and think, "Well, I wasn't given a choice."

You ALWAYS have a choice.

You have the choice to decide how you will live this life.

You can live as a victim or take responsibility for your life.

The moment you decide you are responsible, you give yourself POWER.

Think of this body as a vessel to carry you through this life.

If you do not take care of your vessel, then it will be more prone to break down.

Even for your car to function properly, it must be serviced every 3,000-5,000 miles.

You also have to drive it regularly while also putting the correct fuel in it.

If a car just sits, then it won't operate properly because it must be driven and serviced.

Your body is very similar.

If you don't maintain and service your body, work it, and feed it nourishing food (more of this in Chapter 18) and rest (sleep, meditate, silence, etc.), it will break down.

When I had my first son (who is now 23 years old at the time of this writing), I had a fabulous doctor.

His name was coincidentally Dr. Campbell (but as my husband regularly tells me, there are no coincidences in the realms of the quantum world).

When I would go in for my pre-natal check-ups, he would remind me I was responsible for MY health and the health of my baby while pregnant.

At each checkup, he was a great accountability partner when I gained a bit too much weight.

He encouraged me to continue training while pregnant, which allowed me to stay healthier (mentally, physically and emotionally).

I trained all the way up until I had my son and I felt fabulous throughout my entire pregnancy.

JUST START MOVING - IT DOESN'T HAVE TO BE PERFECT!

What stops you from working your body?

For most, the #1 excuse is no time.

Really?

How much time are you on social media?

How much time do you watch TV?

How much time do you waste laying around?

If you truly want to crack the "Fountain of Youth" code, then working your body must become a priority.

Working your body is a requirement, just like brushing your teeth.

Put it in your schedule and do it.

If you don't use it, you lose it.

Many women have no idea where to begin.

Where do you begin?

Much depends on where you are NOW.

The most important step is to begin.

Remember, you determine where you are and how you want to start.

If anyone knows you best, it is YOU. JUST START.

Time and time again you're told, "check with your doctor when starting any new workout program".

I am not going to tell you to avoid your doctor before starting an exercise program.

Ultimately, you must know what is best for you more than any doctor.

We have gotten to a point where we don't take responsibility for ourselves and we think someone else knows more about us then we do.

Most doctors have hundreds if not thousands of patients.

Do you think they are always thinking of you and how to keep you healthy?

They have their own concerns (ranging from their business to their families and their own health).

If you have any doubts about physical exercise, start low and go slow.

Ask your doctor for permission (especially if you are extremely out of shape), but trust yourself above anyone else.

Are you supremely overweight?

Start doing fasted cardio, meaning don't eat before you do cardio in the morning.

This can be a brisk walk outside, or a walk on a treadmill.

Get your body moving without food.

And when you move, move with intention.

Don't flail your arms around and act like what you are doing is helping.

If you have issues with having to eat first thing in the morning, then eat less.

Just remember to structure a program that works for YOU, based on YOU.

My husband and I have a treadmill and stationary bike in our bedroom to make it easy to do cardio at home.

Any form of cardio is better than none at all.

The older you are, the more important it is to do low-impact cardio because this will preserve your joints, ligaments and tendons as you age.

Running on hard pavement breaks your body down. If you don't have cardio equipment at home, then drive to the gym.

However, having cardio devices in our bedroom makes it easy for us to ensure we do cardio on our non-weight training days.

You are where you are because of the choices YOU'VE made.

If you truly want to change, then YOU must take action to improve.

Make it a priority to Improve your eating and exercise habits.

Doing so will ensure you see results.

WEIGHT TRAINING FOR WOMEN

Weight training (a.k.a. resistance training, or strength training) helps women as they age because it strengthens our bones/bodies.

I recommend all women perform weight/strength training.

How you begin depends on where you are.

If you are extremely overweight and unconditioned, it is important to start slow and avoid lifting heavy weights.

This is crucial because starting slow will help you learn proper form.

Understanding how to train with perfect form is essential to improve your physique.

Additionally, pay attention to your heart rate and how your body is reacting as you are starting off.

Only you can know this.

I am appalled at how many "gym trainers" have overweight people performing exercises that can lead to injury.

Don't let your ego get involved and make you think you have to start lifting heavy.

Use the lightest weight possible until you can get the form down (no "jerky" movements).

Additionally, use slow and controlled movements.

Eliminate momentum and poor form from your training.

Feel the muscle being worked and learn how to forcibly contract your muscle fibers.

Breathe while doing the exercise.

There is so much power in controlling your breath when performing strength training exercises.

As time goes on and your form improves, increase the weight gradually (pay attention to form).

I like to think of weight training as a form of meditation.

I focus on my breath and contracting the muscle during the movement of the exercise.

I feel every part of my muscle contracting, and then slowly release.

It's a fun way to get in sync with my body.

You can also begin with resistance bands.

There are all kinds of different workouts on YouTube.

However, I don't recommend "CrossFit" for newbies.

Many of the exercises are explosive and momentum-based.

They pose a high risk for injury if not performed properly.

CrossFit is popular, but injuries are normal due to its explosive and ballistic nature.

Use caution if you are going to do it.

Above all else, please understand that you don't have to go to the gym every day to lift weights.

You can even buy light weights or resistance bands, and train at home.

As you get more comfortable, the natural progression is to eventually join a gym.

Don't join a gym to act like you will go and never use your membership.

And by all means, a weight training workout should never take longer than 60 minutes.

This ultimately depends on how many people you are training with.

If it takes you longer than 60 minutes, you are socializing, distracted or likely glued to your phone.

If you're not focused on your training, your results will suffer.

If you really want this to become a lifestyle, set yourself up to win!

Schedule your exercise.

As I said before, make this a part of who you are.

I will train with my husband 3 to 4 days a week, and switch up our training regimen 2-3 times a year depending on our fitness goals.

We follow all the advice already given.

We also use proper technique and slow, controlled movements.

My husband has very advanced knowledge about resistance training and lifting weights productively.

In his newest book, Living A Fully Optimized Life: How to Break Free from Sick Care Medicine Before It Kills You, he has an entire chapter about everything one would need to learn how to train productively.

He will be launching a resistance training program for aging men and women in early 2020.

To find out much more about it, go here: www.pmfsystem.com

We never go above 90 minutes for a session.

We ALWAYS fit our workouts in despite our extremely busy schedules.

CARDIOVASCULAR EXERCISE FOR WOMEN

Please, please, PLEASE limit running on streets or hard pavement.

You will destroy your body over time[8].

---

8 http://fabfitover40.com/2014/10/10/running-and-cardio-can-lead-life-wheel chair/

Many people love the "runner's high" associated with running.

I also loved the high, but my knees remind me of why running on hard surfaces is no good for my joints.

If you choose to run outside, then perhaps run on tracks or dirt trails (pay attention to the terrain while running outside).

I prefer a StairMaster or Treadmill, which allows me to read as I do cardio (i.e. cardiovascular exercise).

Some people have a hard time reading while doing this kind of cardio, but for me it works.

Find something that works for you (Zumba Class, a Spin Class, a stationary exercise bike, swimming, etc.).

Just make sure it's low-impact cardio to preserve your soft joints and soft tissues.

And when you're doing cardio, work up a sweat.

You can also perform interval training to get a good sweat going (while paying attention to your heart rate).

Make it fun for yourself so you actually want to do it.

Don't go into it with the attitude that you hate it, or that it is an inconvenience.

You will simply be defeating the purpose of doing cardio, and end up not doing it.

Don't flail around when doing cardio.

Be intentional with your cardio and training.

It will allow you to have more productive results.

I like to do cardio for 20-60 minutes depending on my schedule.

Jay and I will use vacations as a way to push ourselves and get in even better shape.

When we get close to a vacation or we have a photoshoot coming up, we do fasted cardio in the morning and a second cardio session later in the day.

For more information on fasted cardio, my husband has written two amazing books, "The Metabolic Blow Torch Diet" (more for newbies and people unfamiliar with fasting for fat loss) and Guaranteed Shredded (which is written for advanced dieters and people who want to achieve 'ripped' status).

Both are tremendous resources for reducing your body fat in the fastest, safest and most effective way possible.

YOGA FOR WOMEN

Yoga is a fabulous way for you to stay in shape (physically, emotionally, and spiritually).

Don't let your lack of flexibility stop you from attempting this.

It is like anything else: The more you practice, the better you will become.

Yoga teaches you about breathing and being present with your body.

It truly is a beautiful experience.

There are so many different options with a yoga class.

You can join one online, or go in person to a studio.

There are many free videos online for you to view at a time that's convenient for you while at home.

When my kids were younger, I would wake up early and play a yoga DVD in to get my yoga time in.

If you can, go to a class.

It is a great way to truly be present and work your body, as home workouts can come with lots of distractions.

For me, yoga helps me to get my physical and emotional kinks out.

There are plenty of other types of workouts.

Do one that works for you.

If you enjoy boxing, then do it!.

Just WORK your body!

💡 TIPS FOR CRACKING THE CODE: WORK YOUR BODY

1 - Get a workout partner if it helps you actually train.

If you will be distracted and socialize more, then go solo.

Go on the scheduled days no matter what, even if you don't feel like it.

It is important to make it a habit.

If you are sick or just don't want to get out of bed, do your best and drive to the gym.

Even if you just sit in your car and journal for a bit, at least you are allowing yourself to stick to your schedule.

If you can train at home, then actually train at home.

Don't use your exercise equipment as a way to hang your clothes until they're dry.

2 - If you have a desk job, do your best to stand every 30-45 minutes.

The longer you sit, the more your posture will suffer.

If you are sitting, do little exercises as you sit.

For example, squeeze your butt cheeks and release them a couple of times.

It's good for your body and your mind to take occasional standing breaks.

After all, sitting down for long periods of time can make us feel lethargic and unmotivated.

3 - Before you train, set an intention of how you want your training session to evolve.

Visualize your best self coming out, feeling energized and ready to take on the day.

Imagine yourself completing each and every rep with perfect form and laser focus (if you're doing weight training).

If you're doing cardio, visualize yourself completing the workout with maximum energy and a smile across your face.

4 - Walk more.

Park in the furthest parking spot possible so you'll have to walk a bit further.

Take your dogs for walks (They will love you for it. The word "walk" is the only word that causes our dogs to get excited).

Walk with your kids.

Go on a hike.

Just move your body.

5 - Instead of going to Starbucks, save money and buy a treadmill (or whatever low-impact cardio device floats your boat) to put in your home.

This makes it easy for for you to do fasted cardio morning and get a head start on your day.

Save your money to buy this.

Don't get into debt to buy equipment, as it will only cause you to stress more (and who wants added wrinkles?).

6 - Buy an outfit at the size you want to be.

Hang it up where you will see it every day.

Try it on from time to time.

Get excited about the possibility of wearing it.

Visualize what you would look like wearing it.

Imagine how good it will feel on your body when it fits you just right without any discomfort.

CHAPTER 18
FOOD

"When you truly understand that your food choices are powerful and life affirming, you can exercise control and restraint without deprivation"
–Marlene Adelmann

We are all grown women.

In this chapter, I will be speaking to you as such.

I am not an expert when it comes to food and nutrition.

I am an expert when it comes to knowing which foods are most productive for MY body.

Do you know which foods are most productive for your body?

My intention in this chapter is to awaken your mind and help you approach food from a different perspective.

I won't be offering you a fad diet.

To me, they are lame and don't work.

There are plenty of fad diets.

There is a diet for almost everything.

I honestly cannot even keep track of how many diets there are.

Diets don't fail, people do.

Women will start a diet they won't follow.

They eventually fail and gain all their weight back plus more.

Do not start a diet you won't follow long term.

Let's be real.

Food is a drug.

Food is THE most addictive drug in the world.

Look at how many people in the world are now considered obese.

It has become the new normal to be overweight.

Many women are addicted to certain foods and (in their mind) have no control over what they eat.

If anything must improve, it is how and what we eat.

It is also understanding the control that food has over us.

Want to look and feel better as you age?

Be more active and put less food in your mouth.

It IS simple, and yet we make it SO difficult.

We live in a time where food can be the enemy because so many options are available to us.

Although we have so many options, we have no idea how to exercise control.

We can eat almost anything at any time.

Plus, food tastes SO good.

Food often helps us feel happy.

Food is used as a way to bring people together.

Celebrations are centered around food.

Food is a way to show people we care about them.

At least, that is what we tell ourselves.

But what if we viewed food in a different way?

Instead, what if we viewed food as fuel, rather than an emotional crutch?

We all have the same amount of time in a given day, but our habits have created the illusion that we don't have time to eat healthy.

No time to prepare.

No time to shop.

No time to plan.

That all stops at this moment!

You are reading this book because you have decided to take full control over your life.

You know that you are powerful.

You know food is just your fuel.

You know you decide what you pick up and put in your mouth.

You know there are certain "feel good" foods you must limit.

So let's do it then!

MINDFUL EATING HABITS TO START PRACTICING TODAY

Let's start with something simple.

If it is in a box, don't eat it.

Or limit the amount you do eat of it.

Do your best to eat foods made fresh.

FOOD

As we get older, we don't need as much food to fuel our body.

Just eat less!

If you don't weight train in the morning, then fast until lunch time (if this is healthy for you).

If you do weight train in the morning or sometime during the day, eat something that will fuel your body for training (oatmeal, eggs, and low glycemic carbs are good choices).

But don't eat too much, as you will feel like you want to barf after training.

At night, STOP munching.

Stop eating at least 3 hours before you go to bed.

You are doing yourself NO good if you are stuffing your face right before bed.

This makes your body work harder at processing the food you ate instead of allowing it to regenerate and heal as it is intended to do.

Late night snacks are more of a habit than a necessity.

If you have a habit of snacking late at night, it is most likely because you have a habit (like watching TV) you have grown accustomed to as you do it.

Do NOT wake up in the middle of the night to grab food.

STOP watching TV.

Do late night cardio.

Go for a walk.

Do something different to break the habit of sitting and stuffing your face.

Switch up this habit for at least a month to give yourself evidence it can be done.

YOU ARE THE ONE CHOOSING TO CREATE THESE HABITS.

STOP PLAYING VICTIM TO FOOD.

FOOD HAS NO CONTROL OVER YOU EXCEPT THE POWER YOU GIVE IT.

From the moment we were children, we have ingrained beliefs about food.

Perhaps you were rewarded for doing a good thing by having ice cream.

Now every time something great happens in your life, you fill up on ice cream.

Perhaps you are from a Mexican family (like me) and you have happy memories around family gatherings.

These events supplied an unlimited supply of chips, guacamole, salsa, enchiladas, rice and refried beans (pure saturated lard) with going back for seconds and thirds.

In your current life, you like to gather family, serve loads of 'comfort foods', and stuff yourself to the point where you feel like you can't walk.

It can become a habitual process passed down from one generation to the next.

Fortunately, we have wonderful resources to teach us about nutrition and the clean healthy food options available to us.

Unfortunately, most of us can't handle the power and freedom we were given.

It really is as simple as understanding your own body.

Listen to your body after you eat certain foods.

Do you feel sluggish?

Do you get an upset stomach?

Do you feel energized after you eat?

Your body will give you feedback after you eat certain foods.

Why do you think some people get an allergic reaction to eating certain kinds of food?

Because their body is giving them feedback.

If you know certain foods do not agree with you, DON'T eat them.

Let's rephrase that.

If your body tells you certain foods don't agree with it, then don't eat them.

If your mind tells you that certain healthy foods don't agree with you (such as vegetables), then change the way you look at vegetables.

CONTROLLING YOUR PORTIONS, ONE PLATE AT A TIME

How much we eat is also key.

In the United States, our portions have gotten out of control.

If you were raised like I was, you were taught to eat everything on your plate.

"There are people out there starving in the world!"

People fill up their plates (over-filling them with food) and most will eat all the food on their plates.

We do the same to our kids who only take a few bites off their plate, and what they don't eat is thrown out.

If we could package up all the food wasted every day and feed it to the hungry, world hunger would likely be eliminated.

A QUICK NOTE FOR VEGANS AND VEGETARIANS

If you are a vegetarian or vegan, then make sure you are getting a good source of protein every day.

I know plenty of vegetarians and vegans who are not healthy because they have no idea how to properly nourish their bodies, (i.e. consume enough essential amino acids for healthy brain and muscle functioning).

Their main focus has been more on NOT eating meat or any form of animal protein.

They have not been focused on proper nourishment for their body.

If you are a vegetarian/vegan who does know how to properly nourish your body, AWESOME!

What many vegans/vegetarians mistakenly do is eat things like tofu (made from soy) and processed carbs, both of which ARE NOT healthy.

Don't get so caught up on being a vegetarian or vegan that you don't listen to your body and discover what is best for you!

Yes, you can be strong being a vegetarian or vegan if you are eating, resting and training properly.

However, there are people who simply like to speak about themselves being vegetarian or vegan, and how difficult it is to find food they can eat.

Many vegans often complain how no one at gatherings thinks about them when food is cooked.

If you choose to be a vegetarian or vegan, then good for you!

It is no one else's responsibility to ensure you eat properly but yours.

You have made a choice about how you want to eat.

It doesn't mean the world has to cater to your needs.

Luckily, more and more people are becoming vegetarian and/or vegan, so more options are available to you.

Here are some quick tips I have for you…

First, get rid of the following foods:

<u>Anything in a box</u> (except water in a box) – Eat fresh as much as possible.

<u>White sugar</u> is a poison and is SUPER addictive.

There is SO much sugar in food (high fructose corn syrup, etc.) that it is challenging to get rid of sugar all together.

If you can, then my hat is off to you.

But most people would do better if they just limited their sugar intake.

It's hard to drop something completely when it has been an active part of your life.

Therefore, as a starting point, begin limiting it more and more.

<u>White flour</u> is also not very good either.

Begin limiting it more and more until you can eliminate it from your diet (I still haven't completely eliminated it yet).

<u>Fried foods</u> should also be limited.

Do your best to avoid frying your foods in "partially hydrogenated" oils.

Use pure extra virgin olive oil and coconut oil (some say that coconut oil is not good, but I love it) if you must fry.

Sadly, food has become a drug for many women.

We can find so many reasons why we must eat chocolate, chips, breads, crackers, cheese, ice cream, drink soda, and the list goes on:

- *I am on my period*
- *I am PMS-ing*

- *I am stressed*
- *I am watching a movie*
- *I am bored*
- *I am craving [insert junk food here]…*
- *I can't survive unless I have a big breakfast.*
- *I don't want to get hangry.*

We have developed a belief about our eating patterns.

Because of these beliefs, food controls us.

Please listen to me…

YOU HAVE CONTROL OVER WHAT YOU PUT IN YOUR MOUTH.

YOU ARE THE ONE WHO LIFTS YOUR HAND TO PUT THE FOOD IN YOUR MOUTH.

YOU ARE THE ONE WHO KEEPS EATING EVEN WHEN YOU ARE FULL.

If you don't understand that you have the power to change your eating habits, then you will never change your eating habits.

They are only HABITS, and ones YOU CAN CHOOSE to change.

Remember: FOOD IS FUEL, NOT YOUR CRUTCH.

Gain your goddess power back and decide what goes into your mouth.

HOW TO ACTUALLY EAT HEALTHY FOODS

Once you know what foods work best for you, then pre-plan your foods.

Here's what I mean.

Make your food – or at least lunch for the week – and package them (i.e. have them ready to go) in your fridge.

It makes it easier for you to have your food accessible.

You will be far less likely to snack on things you know are not good for you.

We tend to reach for the easy snacks when they are right in front of us.

Ideally, you won't have foods in your home that tempt you.

But often times, your kids will eat junk food and it will be in your pantry.

If you do the shopping, do your best to stock your home with clean and nutrient-dense foods.

I have found having a fresh dinner helps to mix it up so we don't get tired of having the same foods all the time.

At dinner time, have a protein with a green vegetable and a clean carbohydrate source (ex. Rice, beans, legumes, yams) if you aren't attempting to lean out.

While eating, chew your food and enjoy it.

Enjoy the time you are eating.

Do not sit down and eat while watching TV.

This is an easy way to overeat and get into a habit of having to stuff your face while watching TV.

Get your face out of a screen whenever you eat.

Eat to enjoy eating.

Taste the food and allow yourself to feel like you have had enough without feeling like you have to stuff yourself.

Once you are done with dinner, clean up with your family.

If you are solo, put on good music and have fun cleaning up.

Don't go back into the kitchen and snack.

STAY PROPERLY HYDRATED AT ALL TIMES

I only drink water (except for my occasional Chai Tea Latte).

I put it in a copper container to avoid harmful plastic and its various contaminants.

In my opinion, we drink way too many fruit juices/smoothies, sodas, alcoholic beverages, and anything else besides water.

Think about what you drink.

If it is something other water, how many calories and sugar do you think you consume on a daily basis?

I would be willing to bet that it's quite a LOT of calories and sugar.

Water is THE best liquid to consume as it is the elixir of life itself.

All else is just fluff or "feel-good" liquid.

I won't go into all the benefits of water, because if you are breathing then you know water is what is best for you to drink.

You don't, however, because you want to "feel" good for the moment.

Yet ironically, drinking water helps you feel good in the long term.

Don't like the taste of water?

Add lemon or cucumber to the water.

You can add plenty of things to water so it tastes better.

But be cautious of what you add and how much of it.

Don't add ingredients that do your body no good.

If you are going to eat or drink anything that you know is not good for you, then don't continue to beat yourself up mentally.

Do your best to eat it with a smile and improve your self-control the next time you eat.

Bless the food/drink as it goes into your body (after all, we are all energy).

A blessing is positive energy, so infuse the crappy food with a blessing.

At the very least, you won't have guilt running through your body, which can deplete you even further.

Just realize that if your diet is consistently crappy food, not even a true sage could bless it in a way to fuel your body.

The goal is to never play victim to food.

You can bless alcohol all you want, but my theory is that it's called "spirits" for a reason (so you can get some other spirits coming to you from the alcohol).

It could take a whole village of praying for you to get rid of those unwanted "spirits".

My suggestion: Limit alcohol intake, especially if you want to look and feel younger.

And by all means, don't smoke if you want to truly feel and look younger.

Smoking is a sure way to age and kill you.

A SUPER-SHORT OVERVIEW OF FASTING/CLEANSING

Intermittent fasting has become very popular and everyone seems to have a trick about how to do it correctly.

(For an actual way on doing it better, follow my husband's plan in "The Metabolic Blow Torch Diet").

Fasting has many benefits from a health, cognitive, and spiritual perspective.

Fasting takes discipline because our habits tell our mind we are hungry, even if we aren't.

Our habits make us think we will go hungry if we don't eat by a certain time.

If you can get good at fasting, then you can get good at almost anything.

Fasting can even help you respect food more.

Having a better emotional relationship with food will help many, many women.

Think about knowing you don't "NEED" to eat.

You know you can hold off until a certain time when your fast is over.

Whoa...that takes supreme power!

This is when you know you can use food for fuel.

It can start with simply not eating after 7pm one night, and then not eating until the next day at 3 pm.

This is a 20 hour fast.

The key is to not stuff yourself with crappy food after you break your fast.

When you do start eating (i.e. break the fast), eat a protein and green vegetable, especially if you have a significant amount of body fat to lose.

Fasting is great for healing sickness too.

Most diseases and sickness feed off the crap we put into our bodies.

When we stop feeding our bodies crap, the disease or sickness can't feed.

It sounds simple, yet most people discount it because it is.

Most people don't want to admit that they helped to create and feed a sickness in their own body.

Take responsibility for what your body is going through to empower yourself to move past any sickness.

This means taking responsibility for what you choose to put in your body.

Eating foods which make your body feel stronger will help you age better.

Your body won't have to work so hard at processing the food, and it will use the extra energy to replenish life-enhancing cells.

DEALING WITH BODY INSECURITIES AND "FLAWS"

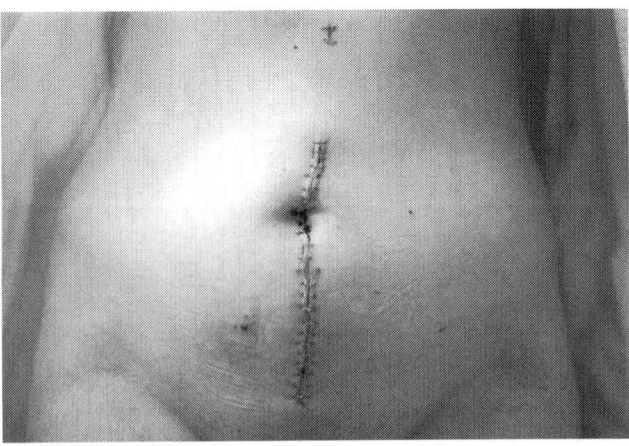

Can you believe there are women out there who hyper focus on what is wrong with their bodies?

YUP!

According to the Anxiety and Depression Association of America[9], Body Dysmorphic Disorder (BDD) is:

"...people who think about their perceived flaws for hours each day.

They can't control their negative thoughts and don't believe people who tell them they look fine.

Their thoughts may cause severe emotional distress and interfere with their daily functioning.

They may even miss work or school, avoid social situations and isolate themselves, even from family and friends, because they fear others will notice their flaws."

Body dysmorphia can cause women to become anorexic or bulimic.

Many women who are anorexic or bulimic don't really know they are, because when they look at themselves, they see a "fat" person even though they are physically fading away.

If you eat very little, or hyper focus on NOT eating, then you are also allowing food to control you (in a different way).

You are resisting food and the essential nutrients it provides your body.

This is a form of self-loathing.

RESPECT your body and know food is fuel.

All high-performance vehicles require THE best type of fuel.

Seek help.

Go to a qualified therapist.

---

[9] https://adaa.org/understanding-anxiety/related-illnesses/other-related-conditions/body-dysmorphic-disorder-bdd

Begin to love yourself more each day. When you haven't loved yourself for so long, how does one begin?

Start small.

Perhaps begin by looking at what you can like about your body.

Do you have your fingers and toes? Are you able to see and/or hear? Do you have skin that covers your body?

Some of these things can sound so simple, and yet there are so many people who have lost their fingers/toes/limbs and learned how to love themselves no matter what.

There are people who don't see or hear, but they love their lives because it is what they know.

KNOW you have value.

Look at your body with eyes of LOVE.

You are worthy to provide your body with the best fuel.

REMEMBER: FOOD IS FUEL, NOT YOUR CRUTCH.

TIPS FOR CRACKING THE CODE: FOOD

1 - Eat out less often.

When you do choose foods, choose the foods you know are better for you.

Ask for smaller portions or share an order with someone.

We really don't need as much food as most of us are accustomed to eating.

We only believe this to be the case because of our past habits and cultural conditioning (from media, our family and friends, etc.).

2 - Bless or pray over your food and drink.

Send it some positive energy so it can properly fuel your body.

Be grateful for the opportunity to provide your body with the nourishment and fuel it needs to be active.

This may sound weird, but you may even find your food tastes better when you start blessing it!

3 - Stop going to your favorite juice bar (or coffee/tea place) so much during the week.

Make it a once a week treat or - even better - once every other week.

You have no idea how many calories and sugars you are putting into your body with all those drinks.

While you might not "feel" like you consumed a lot, your body is going to say otherwise when it leaves you feeling sluggish and bloated.

When in doubt, ALWAYS go with water!

4 - Stop determining your health by how much you weigh.

Start going by how you feel and how your clothes fit.

I weigh the same as when I was pregnant with my kids, but I also have more muscle on my body now.

I rarely weigh myself and mainly check out of curiosity, not because I am attempting to get at a certain weight.

Many women who strength train find they weigh the same as when they started.

However, they end up looking much better because they gained lean muscle while losing body fat!

5 - Don't set a meal plan you won't follow.

Improve what you are doing and do something you know you will follow.

Set yourself up to win, not to lose.

If you keep failing in the food area, then food will always control you.

You have power over what goes in your mouth.

Don't let your mind, mouth, hands and stomach tell you otherwise.

6 - If you have kids, don't buy crappy foods that you know will tempt you.

Get them on the bandwagon of "FOOD IS FUEL."

Many poor eating habits we have today are the direct result of how our parents fed us as kids.

Taking a proactive approach towards nutrition with your kids sets them up for healthy eating habits well into their adult lives.

7 - Eat for YOU!

When some people start a new diet, they want everyone to know what they are doing.

Remember, you are doing this for you.

You don't have to prove to anyone how great you are because you are following a diet.

8 - Be kind to yourself if you cheat.

Let's be real.

We all have eaten foods we know we are not supposed to eat.

I have grabbed chocolate chip cookies when I am supposed to be super disciplined for a vacation or photoshoot.

The way I see it, it does no good to beat myself up for eating the cookie.

I would rather enjoy it and work to do better next time.

Do your best to ACTUALLY improve.

Making excuses all the time for not being in integrity with yourself will cause more harm than good.

CHAPTER 19
HORMONES

"The secret of change is to focus all your energy, not on fighting the old, but on building the new"
–Socrates

When my mom was alive, she didn't want to be on hormone therapy.

She was scared of the side effects she would have because of hormone therapy.

I recall her fearing what hormone therapy could do to her body and state of mind.

Most women are not properly educated on what happens to their hormones as they get older.

I understand many women's desire to deal with aging in the most natural way possible.

The challenge we have is that our world is no longer "natural".

We are depleting the natural resources of our Mother Earth and spreading chemicals everywhere.

Knowing this, aging without hormone therapy could cause you to suffer needlessly.

How would you know?

First of all, how are you feeling as you age?

Do you feel less energetic and tired?

Do you feel irritable?

Are you experiencing hot flashes?

It's important for you to know what you are experiencing.

My suggestion would be to improve lifestyle choices first (removing alcohol, reducing sugar, improving your diet and/or fasting, exercise, etc.).

I would also look into hormone optimization therapy (HOT), which can help ensure your lifestyle choices are the most productive as you age.

WHAT YOU NEED TO KNOW ABOUT HORMONE THERAPY TO GET STARTED

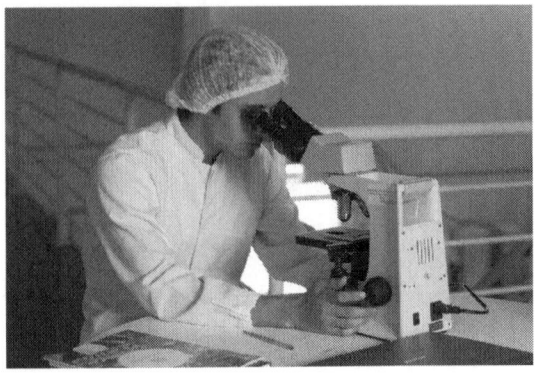

It's important for you to understand that hormone therapy by itself will not help you deal with the effects of aging if you aren't willing to address all the other lifestyle factors previously listed in this book.

I know women unwilling to let go of emotional trauma, and yet they think hormone therapy will cure them.

Hormone therapy won't cure any of your issues if you aren't willing to heal.

You must deal with your emotional trauma and heal to age effectively and properly utilize hormone therapy.

In the past, when women wanted to feel important and noticed, we allowed drugs like birth control pills to be given to us.

This was done without proven clinical studies that demonstrated the potential long-term effects of said drugs on their bodies and their children.

Whether you are for or against birth control, the fact remains that long-term birth control pill usage can adversely impact a woman's body.

Anytime you ingest something (long-term) that is unnatural to your body, your body can and will respond negatively.

Many women are beginning to see these negative side effects as they age.

Since each woman has had different life experiences and choices, the side effects will vary.

On top of the various drugs we have taken over our lifetime, we live in a poisoned environment contaminated by plastics and their byproducts.

We're constantly being exposed to electromagnetic fields (EMF's) from technology, pollution, and more.

In fact, as my husband continually cries out on his podcast, our biological systems are under siege from modern day living.

For this reason, hormone therapy is crucial for many women as we age.

But where do we start?

Find a doctor who specializes in hormone therapy.

While your regular family doctor can attempt to treat you, it takes a true expert with an experiential practice of optimizing women's hormones to help you.

It takes a doctor who understands the finer nuances of manipulating a woman's endocrine system to achieve optimization.

This type of doctor knows how to properly read blood lab reports and can accurately determine which medication would be best suited for you (if any).

A great hormone therapy doctor will most likely be cash pay because insurance companies and health maintenance organizations (HMO's) are reluctant to reimburse for therapy still not understood from an established clinical perspective.

The insurance companies are still the driving force of how doctors deal with their patients.

Additionally, the majority of family doctors have not caught up with what is best for their patient when it comes to hormone optimization therapy.

If you go to your normal 'family' doctor so your insurance can cover it, double check any information they give you.

Most HMO/insurance-covered doctors tend to answer to the insurance and/or pharmaceutical companies, not their patients.

I found this out the hard way.

I attempted to go to one of these doctors in my area.

They had no idea how to deal with me.

They were steering me to what was recommended by their pharmaceutical rep.

Unfortunately, many aging women experience this treatment from their primary care or family doctor.

I trusted my gut and didn't follow their advice.

I found out later from true experts that their advice was not in my best interest.

I haven't been back to that medical group since and will never go there again.

If you really want to understand how your body works, then get a basic understanding of how to read your blood hormone panel.

This will be your "blueprint" on how you are aging.

Jay and I get our blood work done twice a year to make sure we have a clear internal diagnostic.

I review the results with our doctor and determine if I need medications to help me feel and perform better.

It is important to keep track of how I feel, rather than hyper-focus on what my laboratory report and respective biomarkers show.

If I am given a prescription, I take what is directed but I listen to my body.

If I don't feel optimal after taking it, then I lower the dose or eventually stop taking the medication altogether.

Again, my goal is to trust myself first.

At the time of this writing, my periods are hit and miss.

Throughout most of my life, my periods have been 5-7 days with heavy flow for the first 2 days.

In the past, I have been prescribed testosterone cream and progesterone.

The testosterone cream made me break out, so I stopped taking it.

The progesterone made me feel too tired, so I stopped taking it.

Instead, I listen to what my body is telling me.

DEALING WITH MENOPAUSE AS WE AGE

Menopause can actually be a beautiful transition for women if we view it as such.

Sadly, most of us are taught to fear menopause.

- *Will I still be valuable?*
- *Will I still be attractive?*
- *Will I be old because of menopause?*
- *Will I have hot flashes?*
- *Will I lose my hair?*
- *Will I go crazy?*

It is like even the word is warning men.

Afterall, look at the word: "Men...O...Pause".

Yo Men! O, Pause, she is angry!

It's interesting how we can make a word mean anything based on how we have been conditioned.

There are many concerns which can often pop into our minds, making menopause a chapter in our lives we wish we could avoid.

What if we could celebrate the different chapters in life instead?

I like to view menopause as graduating into the sage realm.

Our bodies move away from producing life and move into a segment of birthing true wisdom into the world (if we allow ourselves to go within).

It truly is a beautiful time for women.

What if we could actually celebrate menopause and embrace it?

Create something fun, or a way to commemorate moving into your sage years.

You can have a special ceremony with other women in your circle, have a weekend getaway by yourself, or something special you can anchor the memory with.

You are moving into a new chapter of your life.

Honor it.

Appreciate it.

Every segment of our life depends on how we view it.

If you go into menopause dreading it, you will likely manifest "side effects".

Remember: The universal mirror is always in effect.

We always get back what we reflect.

Getting older is admittedly not easy because we might slow down.

Allowing it to stop us is a choice.

If you are a worrier, then your menopause symptoms will be more pronounced.

Be the observer in your life instead.

Observe how you feel and notice what is working best for you.

Your beauty or worth does not fade because you are in menopause.

Menopause is simply defined as when a woman stops having her period.

Think about it.

No more wearing tampons or thick pads.

No more having to concern yourself with whether or not you bleed through an outfit.

There is so much more to celebrate about menopause than there is to resist.

Allow menopause to flow into your life, just like your menstrual cycle used to.

Perhaps women are meant to be flowing throughout their life?

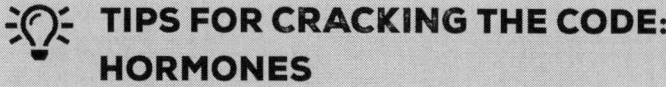
TIPS FOR CRACKING THE CODE: HORMONES

1 - Are you noticing changes in your body?

Your periods are hit and miss, and your body just doesn't feel the same.

Ask yourself and your body about the ways you can honor it during this time.

Perhaps it is through rest.

Perhaps it is through exercise.

Perhaps it is through meditation.

Invest time to listen, and then take positive action to improve.

2 - Love yourself now more than ever.

Appreciate your changing body.

Realize you have lived in multiple bodies throughout your lifetime.

At one time you were an itty-bitty baby, then a toddler, then a tween, then a teenager, then an adult.

Now, you are an older woman.

Welcome this woman with eyes of love.

3 - Play around with different looks.

Your hair may be falling out at a quicker pace.

Don't allow yourself to stress over it.

Cut it short or wear a wig from time to time.

Being in resistance about your body "falling apart" will only have it fall apart faster.

What you resist most assuredly persists.

4 - Wear comfortable shoes.

Luckily, we now have shoes that can be sexy and comfy.

Wearing 6-inch-high heels all the time surely doesn't help our feet feel good.

Look at ways to bring added comfort into your life.

You also don't have to wear "old woman" shoes.

Wear what makes you feel good and allows you to move around easily.

5 - Research Jade Egg's or Secret Ceres to see if they can help you stay in touch with (and strengthen) your feminine parts.

6 - As soon as you open your eyes, tell yourself how happy you are to be alive.

Before you go to bed, tell yourself how grateful you are to have had another day.

Fill your day and night with blessings.

Every single night before we go to bed, both my husband and I say a form of this prayer:

> *Dear God, Angels and Guides,*
>
> *I request to attend the most evolved place I may move to with my consciousness, for the purpose of clarity about my mission, my purpose and service.*

Let me learn and understand better what I need to achieve my fullest potential.

Please assist me in any upgrades that may be possible.

Notice all of the lessons and accomplishments you have racked up to this day - combined, they have helped you become the wise and wonderful woman that you are today.

7 - Feeling a bit tired? Get a helping hand!

Delegate things for others to do.

Be ok with other people helping you.

Your self-worth and value do not diminish in any way because you have sought out help from others.

If anything, it allows you to embrace your own strengths while honoring those of other people.

We all bring something unique to this game we call "life".

CHAPTER 20
SLEEP

"Sleep is the golden chain that binds health and our bodies together"
-Thomas Dekker

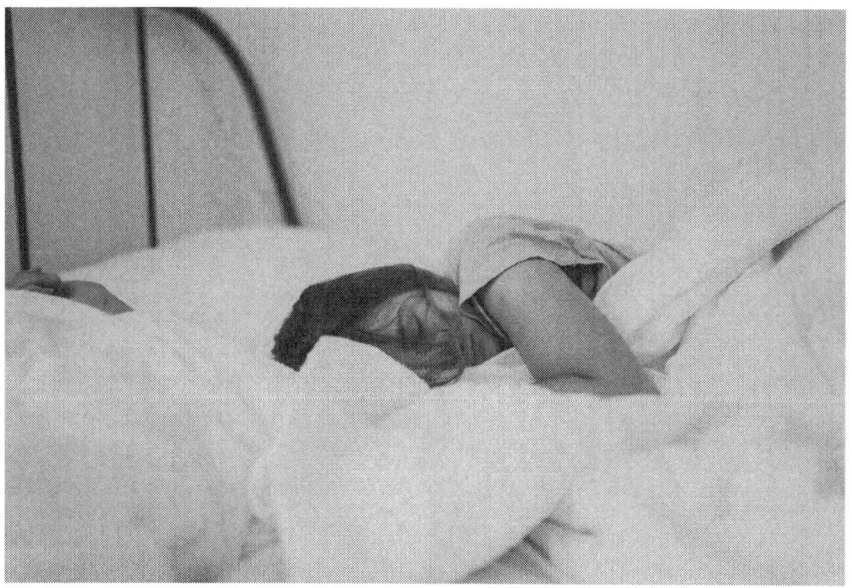

Have you ever gone without sleeping one night?

Two nights?

Three nights or longer?

Continuous lack of sleep can cause your body to break down.

Sleep is when your body heals and regenerates.

Sleep also allows your mind to rest.

Not only will sleepless nights bring tired eyes, but your body and mind will also suffer.

When I was in my 30's, I was part of a coaching organization where my mentor would say time and time again,

"Work! You can sleep when you're dead".

I cringe when I think of that statement as I now realize how important sleep is.

It seems much of the debate about sleep is exactly how much we need every night.

Rather than asking how much sleep I recommend, I suggest you gauge how you feel after a certain amount of deep, uninterrupted sleep.

We want to add up our hours of sleep, and we are generally happy when we sleep 7 hours through the night.

But if your sleep is interrupted, your sleep is not deep or restful.

Remember: You are YOU, and other people are other people.

Just because one person states they cannot survive without 8 hours of sleep doesn't mean that you can't thrive on 5 hours of uninterrupted sleep.

How will you know?

The only surefire way to know is to assess your mood and energy levels throughout the day.

If you did not get enough sleep, then you will feel tired and sluggish by lunch time.

If you slept enough, you will have enough energy to take you through the day.

I like to think of sleep as a time when our soul leaves our body to explore another world.

It is also a time where your unconscious can speak to you through your dreams.

You live a whole different world in your dreams.

Are they real?

Of course they are!

At least while you are dreaming it.

What the mind of (wo)man can believe, it can conceive, right?

DEALING WITH BAD SLEEPING HABITS & THEIR CAUSES

If you have problems with sleep, it can be for several reasons.

As stated in the Grounding chapter, sleep can be affected by our lack of exposure to the earth and its healing components.

Stress can also be a factor, along with your immediate environment and dietary choices.

How will you know what is affecting you?

It's important for you to assess what is going on with you to determine the reason why you are not sleeping well.

In the past, there were times I found it easy to fall asleep.

But if I had to wake up to use the bathroom, my mind would not allow me to fall back to sleep.

My mind would start racing about issues going on in my life and different scenarios would start going through my mind.

Before I knew it, 2 hours would pass and I would still be tossing and turning, unable to sleep.

I would feel bad and get up to go to the couch so I wouldn't wake my husband.

Unfortunately, with my tossing and turning, and then getting up to move to the couch, I would inevitably wake my husband up.

I would then feel bad for waking him up and stay up even longer.

The cycle can be vicious.

In case you haven't noticed, stress is the culprit.

It's allowing my over-active mind to play out situations I have no control of.

If my mind attempts to go into a situation I know will keep me awake, I shift it into a place of peace and sleep.

I don't allow my mind to stay engaged with thoughts that want to scare me.

It takes practice, but it helps for getting a good night's sleep.

We each create our own sleeping patterns, whether you realize it or not.

Most of us will fall asleep around the same time, wake up in the middle of the night around the same time, and wake up in the morning at the same time.

If you truly want to improve your sleep, then pay attention to your sleep patterns.

Observe what wakes you up.

Do you go to the bathroom before bed to empty your bladder before bed time?

Are you drinking lots of liquid just before bed?

Are you overstimulating yourself with blue light (via your smartphone, computer, tablet and/or TV) before bed?

Once you have observed your sleeping patterns, now it is time to create better sleep habits.

I have found napping to be a saving grace for me as I have gotten older.

I don't mean 2-3 hour naps.

I love 15-30 minute naps.

They can give you a little burst of energy to get you through the day.

I love doing guided meditations that help get me into different levels of rest and relaxation without having to fall asleep completely.

These guided meditations allow me to feel energized and ready to go.

They can be anywhere from 20-45 minutes.

You may want to set an alarm to wake up, just in case you fall asleep and have to be somewhere on time.

One final note before I close out this chapter:

You DO NOT need sleeping pills to fall asleep or keep you asleep.

Sleeping pills can cause you to depend on them as a crutch to fall asleep.

They won't allow you to fall into the type of restorative deep sleep that actually heals your body.

Depending on sleeping pills to sleep can actually make you nervous about going to sleep.

Instead, look forward to going to sleep!

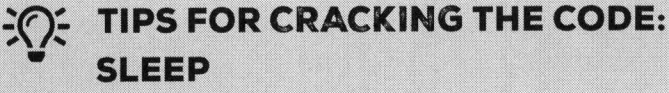 TIPS FOR CRACKING THE CODE: SLEEP

1 - Create productive sleep habits.

Get to bed around the same time and strive to wake up around the same time too.

Make sure your room is as cool as possible and as dark as possible.

Do something relaxing (read a book, meditate, have a bath, etc.) right before you go to sleep.

If needed, invest in some higher-quality sleep equipment (mattress, pillows, grounding pad etc.) to ensure you are more comfortable while sleeping.

2 - Charge your phone outside of the bedroom so you don't have any distractions and are not looking at the phone just before bed.

If possible, try to abstain from using any form of technology at least 1 hour before you go to bed.

In the bedroom I share with my husband, we do not have any technology whatsoever.

The bedroom is for sleeping and sex, nothing else.

If you rely on your smartphone as an alarm, replace it with an old-school alarm clock.

3 - Don't eat right before bed.

A full stomach can make it harder to go to sleep and sleep soundly.

If you are going to eat in the nighttime, try to have your last meal at least 3 hours before you go to bed.

This will give your body plenty of time to digest all the food, allowing you to slip into a more relaxed state when it is time for bed.

4 - Don't drink lots of caffeine.

Being over stimulated can make it harder to fall asleep.

When you have your cup of coffee (or two) for the day, try to keep it in the morning.

If you absolutely have to drink coffee in the afternoon, make sure your last cup is at least 6 hours before your planned bedtime.

5 - Do a brain dump before bed.

Get a pad of paper and write everything down that is bothering you.

After you write it all down, crumble up the paper and toss it away.

As you do that, thank God for taking care of all your problems.

The act of physically writing your thoughts on paper allows them to leave your mind and be placed somewhere else instead.

6 - As you go to sleep, visualize yourself in a soothing environment.

Picture yourself somewhere very relaxing.

Feel like you are there and just sink into the feeling.

Allow yourself to escape into this other world falling asleep.

This takes practice, but with time you will find that you are able to fall into a deeper sleep, faster than ever before.

7 - As you go to sleep, think about all you have to be grateful for.

Fall asleep in full appreciation for your life.

Be thankful for your comfortable mattress, nice pillow, soft blankets and a roof over your head to help you sleep peacefully at night.

Bless all the friends and family in your life who you love and care for.

Cherish the small wins you had in your day.

8 - As you go to sleep, place an energetic field around you.

I do this when I feel like I may be getting sick, or have been hanging out somewhere that depletes my energy.

I mentally scan my body for where it could be affected, and then shine a light in that area.

I mentally place the field around my body, around my room, around my home.

I feel at peace knowing I am protected.

I will also do this with my children if I am concerned for them.

CHAPTER 21
HAVE FUN

*"You don't stop having fun because you get old,
you get old because you stop having fun"*
–Unknown

We have all heard the saying "Life is short, have fun".

Yet how many of us truly enjoy life and have fun?

As women, we can get so caught up in taking care of others that we lose sight of the enjoyment of life.

Life becomes more of a chore than an experience.

Time passes by and before you know it, the years show pieces of evidence on our face and bodies that reflect how tired and depleted we are.

Does life really have to be this way?

NO!

We all have choices.

Even with children, a career, a mate, aging parents, responsibilities, and so on, we can actually enjoy our lives.

Give yourself permission to have some fun.

Have you ever heard the saying, "Laughter is the best medicine"?

If you haven't, then I am telling you that laughter is unquestionably the best medicine.

Who said you have to be so serious when you get older?

I would be willing to bet whoever taught you to be serious 24/7 is probably already dead or miserable.

Don't listen to them.

If you desire to crack the "Fountain of Youth" code, then learn to have some fun!

This doesn't mean throwing away all your responsibilities.

You can have fun and still be responsible.

SOME SHORT YET SIMPLE TIPS FOR HAVING MORE FUN IN YOUR LIFE

Have fun with the little things in life.

If you are at work, smile more.

If you are at home, smile more.

Smiling is contagious and is one way to have more fun.

If you are concerned about wrinkles with smiling, then you aren't having fun.

Some women have forgotten what it is like to smile and have a resting mad face.

Do you mean to tell me a frown is more attractive than a smile?

When was the last time you allowed yourself to actually enjoy yourself at a party, or at an event?

Or simply skip instead of walking?

Do you allow yourself to sing along to songs anymore?

Have you ever closed your eyes and allowed yourself to feel the beat of a tune?

Allow your body to move with the beat and feel the music.

This is so fun!

Have you ever tossed the ball around with your kids or grandkids?

Hearing their little giggles is so fun.

What do you consider fun?

If you can't think of anything, then you have your work cut out for you.

Start experimenting with what brings you joy.

It could be investing time with your children/grandchildren, or hanging out with friends.

Everyone is different.

Some like to immerse themselves into a good book.

Some like to go dancing.

Some like to shop.

There is no right or wrong way to have fun.

It is simply whatever floats your boat and is within your budget.

I love being in nature.

I love dancing to soothing chill house music.

I love investing time with my children and husband.

I love working and contributing to serve other people.

I love being by myself.

I love being mindful.

**I have found what works for me because
I play around with options.**

I have also found that things can change with time.

What I liked 2 years ago doesn't excite me as much.

I keep exploring what fun is to me.

Explore for yourself.

Take a dance class.

Take a painting class.

Go for a walk in nature.

It doesn't have to be expensive.

In all honesty, having fun doesn't have to be doing anything.

You can train yourself to enjoy anything you are doing.

Taking out the trash?

Hum a tune as you take out the trash.

Going grocery shopping?

Enjoy grocery shopping and mentally give gratitude for the many options to choose from. You don't have to grow or kill your own food anymore!

Don't look at it as a chore.

Having fun can be as complex or simple as you decide to make it.

Some people find joy in the complexity of life.

Some people find joy in the simplicity of life.

If you can find joy, I am pretty sure you can have fun.

Give yourself permission to have fun with whatever you are doing because the days go by fast.

When you are on your deathbed (or are dying) do you want to look back at your life filled with regret because life was more of a chore?

Or would you rather look at your life with gratitude because you truly had fun and enjoyed your life?

You get to decide.

TIPS FOR CRACKING THE CODE: HAVING FUN

1 - Stop setting so many conditions for what 'fun' is.

Keep it simple.

There are no rules to this except for the ones that you arbitrarily set for yourself.

What is "fun" for someone else may not be so fun for you, and vice versa.

As long as YOU are having fun, that's all that really matters!

2 - If you are going to watch TV or a movie, watch something funny at least once a week.

If you don't watch TV, go to a comedy club at least once a month.

Strengthen your laughing muscles.

In a world filled with so much negativity and cynicism, it can be difficult to seek out the humor in life.

Having a chuckle or two can sometimes be the remedy you need to turn a frown upside down.

3 - Watch children play.

Allow this to remind you what you enjoyed as a child.

Tap into your inner child and play again, even if it means making mud pies.

Get dirty - it washes off!

Head on over to the playground and swing on the swings.

Watch one of your favorite TV shows from when you were a little girl.

4 - Turn on the music in your home and dance.

Dance because you can.

Dance for yourself.

Close your eyes and feel the music.

If other people are looking at you and judging you, who cares?!

Let them think whatever they want.

Other people's judgments should never stop you from freely expressing yourself.

5 - Hug those you care about.

Hugging is so much fun and feels so good coming from someone you really care about.

When you hug, hug heart-to-heart.

Feel the embrace and send love to the other person.

This is so fun!

Hug your family members, your friends, and anyone else who you would gladly like to receive a hug from too.

6 - Write a book.

This is fun and exhausting - only two more chapters left! :)

CHAPTER 22
CONTRIBUTION (PASS YOUR GODDESS TORCH)

"The best way to find yourself is to lose yourself in the service to others"
-Mahatma Ghandi

Want to truly feel (and possibly look) younger?

The best way to learn something is to teach it.

Contribute to someone else.

Mentor someone.

This doesn't mean to boss someone around.

This means to truly be there for someone and guide them on their path.

With you being an amazing goddess, it will be easy to pass the goddess torch to another woman.

Recognize that by contributing to others, you will impact the world as a whole.

There is no competition when you are a true goddess, for you know we all have value.

You know women are on this earth to make a positive impact.

You know cooperation and unity are far more powerful than competition.

I have witnessed women refuse to pass the torch out of fear of competition.

As you grow wiser, you realize there is never competition.

You understand the best way to positively change the world is one person at a time.

At the same time, as a wise woman, you don't force yourself on anyone.

Be a guide to a young girl or woman who seeks your help.

For if someone truly wants to learn, then they will be a fabulous student.

There are no secrets left in the world.

Truth is divine and always rises to the surface.

Why not share your abundance of knowledge to help others tap into their own power?

Ever have an older woman you would go to for advice, who had an uncanny ability to put things into perspective?

CONTRIBUTION (PASS YOUR GODDESS TORCH)

It helps to have a sounding board to bounce ideas off, or someone you can confide in without judgement.

These women are priceless.

Be this woman to others.

Think about how amazing this world would be if rather than competing against one another, we contributed to one another!

Coming from a place of contribution is empowering.

It helps us realize we are enough and worthy.

We have a true gift to share with the world.

At times, it can be as simple as smiling at another person and not expecting them to react in a certain way.

Other times, it can simply be where we listen to understand, rather than listening to be understood.

There is a saying I live by:

> "People don't care how much you know until they know how much you care."

Don't ask, "what's in it for me" because if you love yourself, you won't do anything that isn't productive.

Learn to step outside of thinking only for yourself.

Spread those beautiful goddess wings and share them with the world.

Don't misunderstand my message.

Never allow yourself to be a doormat or taken advantage of in your life.

Trust your inner knowing to know what is best for you at any given point in your life.

💡 TIPS FOR CRACKING THE CODE: PASS YOUR GODDESS TORCH

1 - If you have a daughter (or more than one), guide and empower them.

Remind them of their beauty.

Not because of what they wear, but because of who they are.

Allow them to see you appreciate your own beauty.

Allow them to see you honor yourself and put yourself first (at times).

Don't live through your daughter.

Allow them the space to be themselves and live their own life.

Be a guide, not a director.

2 - Genuinely compliment other women for something you like.

Too many of us are taught to be critical of one another.

It's very easy to pick out something we don't like about another woman and amplify it.

Instead, cherish the women in your life for all the gifts and talents they bring into the world.

Honor their bodies exactly as they are.

3 - Help someone without them knowing it is you.

Pay for someone's meal or contribute to charity without getting acknowledgement.

Resist the need to be validated and praised in public for good deeds you perform.

Focus on the joy you've brought to someone's life through small favors done out of the goodness of your own heart.

4 - Create your own fun way to help other women.

Start your own organization.

Create your own mastermind.

Be creative!

Remember to NOT make it about you.

Make it about helping and serving others, first and foremost.

Set ground rules to ensure that all discussions are both positive and productive for all group members.

Word of mouth works a lot faster than you would think! ;)

CONCLUSION

Getting older doesn't have to be scary.

You don't have to dread someone asking your age.

You don't have to define yourself by your age.

You don't have to fear what will happen to you as you get older.

You are perfectly evolving into the woman you are.

The only constant in life is change.

If you allow yourself to get comfortable with change, you will accept who you are as you get older.

Even paying the best age management doctor in the world won't prevent you from getting older or dying.

As you've traveled along this journey, I hope you've learned to appreciate the wonder and awe of aging, and your personal evolution through the process.

You are the best source of cracking your "Fountain of Youth" code when you empower yourself to decide how you will age.

You get to decide how you allow life to affect you and what breaks you down.

Know you are valuable, beautiful, and worthy as a woman (young or old).

Enjoy this journey and spread your goddess sparkle to all those fortunate to be in your life.

You have nothing to prove to the world.

Love yourself unconditionally and be the best version of "you".

Be kind to yourself and others.

I don't have to tell you that time moves faster as you get older.

Stop wasting time with regret, guilt and condemnation.

Start building yourself up to age in the most effective, sexy, powerful way you can.

What will your legacy be when you physically leave this earth?

How will you be remembered?

Write your own story.

I am sending you love as you begin this journey from a fully empowered perspective.

Know the beautiful being you are and the WOMAN you're becoming.

CONCLUSION

My heart is filled with joy to have finished this epic journey with you.

I hope we cross paths one day and you can share how you are cracking your own code.

We are all teachers for one another.

Thank you.

I send you each tremendous amounts of love, light and gratitude!

A SINCERE REQUEST

The information found inside this book provides a real path to empowering women of all ages for life.

In order for this book to reach as many people as possible, we're depending on you!

Please do us a huge favor and write an honest review on Amazon.

The more reviews it gets, the more this information will help others just like you escape from the matrix of mainstream conditioning and thought control.

We are sincerely grateful for the time and effort you put into writing a thoughtful review.

Thank you so much for reading **Cracking the Fountain of Youth Code**.

We hope you use this information to transform into your greatest goddess self.

ABOUT THE AUTHORS

Monica Diaz Campbell is a nationally acclaimed real estate sales professional who has sold over $350 million in residential real estate in Southern California as the Co-Founder of The Monica Diaz Team.

Monica is also an award winning figure-fitness and bikini champion, and Co-Founder of Fabulously Fit Over 40, the #1 site online for "Fitness Over 40" information.

Monica is known on social media for her "Monica's Minute" inspirational videos, which encourage women to become the best versions of themselves.

Monica has overcome tremendous hardships leading to breakthroughs in her life.

As an empowered mother of 3 children plus 2 bonus children, she has a keen ability to draw on her past experiences in relating to people from various backgrounds.

Dr. Mickra Hamilton is the CEO of Apeiron Zoh Corporation, a Precision Performance Medicine Ecosystem creating a new paradigm for what is possible for human flourishing.

She is a creative rebel, international speaker and renowned complex systems and human performance master with specialties in the epigenetics of stress, breath sciences and performance mindset.

Mickra recently retired from a 30-year career in the United States Air Force Reserves serving as a Human Performance Subject Matter Expert.

Made in the USA
Middletown, DE
24 January 2020